THEMATIC UNIT
Knights and Castles

Written by Scott T. Walters

Teacher Created Resources, Inc.
6421 Industry Way
Westminster, CA 92683
www.teachercreated.com

©2000 Teacher Created Resources, Inc.
Reprinted, 2005
Made in U.S.A.

ISBN-1-57690-774-0

Edited by
Lorin Klistoff, M.A.

Illustrated by
Chandler Sinnott

Cover Art by
Larry Bauer

Table of Contents

Introduction

Knights and Castles is an engaging whole-language unit. It is designed to be used for children in intermediate grades, though content is also adaptable for older children. In terms of a literature base, two award-winning texts have been selected: *Catherine, Called Birdy*, designed to give a picture of everyday life during the Middle Ages, and *Proud Taste for Scarlet and Miniver*, which tells of castle life and knighthood. In terms of historical information, pages dealing with daily life, castles, knights, and other topics have been included to be read aloud or individually by students.

Each section contains activities which historically frame the story, provide additional explanations, and extend medieval concepts. In addition, the themes in these books are connected to other areas of the curriculum, such as language arts, math, science, social studies, art, and life skills. The activities were planned to overlap and interrelate to provide a holistic approach to the subject.

Intermediate thematic units should be administered with an understanding of the reading activity and ability of the individuals and groups that will participate in the activity. Some classes will move through units more quickly than others, while others may be able to do much of the material independently or in cooperative learning groups. While much of the material is designed to stand alone or to supplement other medieval history curricula, all of the sections could potentially be covered as a single unit. They are designed to cover broad aspects and give students a picture of life during medieval times.

This thematic unit includes the following:

❑ **literature selections**—summaries of two books with related lessons that cross the curriculum

❑ **planning guides**—suggestions for sequencing lessons for every day of the unit

❑ **short tale**—an adaptation of a medieval tale for use as storytelling or drama

❑ **writing ideas**—writing activities that extend across the curriculum

❑ **class decoration and bulletin board ideas**—suggestions for creating bulletin boards and a medieval atmosphere

❑ **curriculum connections**—ideas for language arts, math, science, social studies, art, and life skills

❑ **group projects**—projects to foster cooperative learning and social skills

❑ **culminating activities**—activities that allow students to synthesize their learning and produce products that can be shared by others

❑ **bibliography**—suggested printed books, video, and electronic resources on the theme of medieval history

> **To keep this valuable resource intact so that it can be used year after year, you may wish to punch holes in the pages and store them in a three-ring binder.**

Introduction *(cont.)*

Why a Balanced Approach?

The strength of a whole-language approach is that it involves children in using all modes of communication—reading, writing, listening, observing, illustrating, and doing. Communication skills are interconnected and integrated into lessons that emphasize the whole of language. Balancing this approach is our knowledge that every whole—including individual words—is composed of parts, and directed study of those parts can help a student to master the whole. Experience and research tell us that regular attention to phonics, other word-attack skills, and spelling develops reading mastery, thereby fulfilling the unity of the whole-language experience. The child is thus led to read, write, spell, speak, and listen confidently in response to a literature experience introduced by the teacher. In these ways, language skills grow rapidly, stimulated by direct practice, involvement, and interest in the topic at hand.

Why Thematic Planning?

One very useful tool for implementing a balanced language program is thematic planning. By choosing a theme with correlating literature selections for a unit of study, a teacher can plan activities throughout the day that lead to a cohesive, in-depth study of the topic. Students will be practicing and applying their skills in meaningful contexts. Consequently, they will tend to learn and retain more. Both teachers and students will be freed from a day that is broken into unrelated segments of isolated drill and practice.

Why Cooperative Learning?

Besides academic skills and content, students need to learn social skills. This area of development cannot be taken for granted. Students must learn to work cooperatively in groups in order to function well in modern society. Group activities should be a regular part of school life, and teachers should consciously include social objectives as well as academic objectives in their planning. For example, a group working together to solve a problem may need to select a leader. Teachers should make clear to the students the qualities of good leader-follower group interaction just as they would state and monitor the academic goals of the project.

Four Basic Components of Cooperative Learning

1. *In cooperative learning, all group members need to work together to accomplish the task.*

2. *Cooperative learning groups should be heterogeneous.*

3. *Cooperative learning activities need to be designed so that each student contributes to the group, and individual group members can be assessed on their performance.*

4. *Cooperative learning teams need to know the social as well as the academic objectives of a lesson.*

Catherine, Called Birdy

by Karen Cushman
(HarperTrophy, 1995)

Summary

Catherine, Called Birdy is written as the journal of 14-year-old Catherine and is set in England in the year 1290. Catherine, who is better known by her nickname, Birdy, is the youngest child of a minor lord. Birdy begins the journal reluctantly, being persuaded to begin it by her family who believes that the journal will make her more ladylike.

Early in the novel, Catherine encounters a group of traveling Jews who stayed briefly at her manor and befriends an old Jewish woman who counsels her to be herself. About this time, Birdy also begins to fend off the marriage proposals of a series of suitors whom her father invites to the manor. He wants her to marry the richest suitor he can find and does not care whether she agrees with his choice or not. Birdy's mother is sympathetic but believes that Birdy should accept her destiny and marry the suitor whom her father chooses. This is the main conflict of the novel.

One suitor, whom Birdy calls "Shaggy Beard," gets dangerously close to marrying her. He offers a set of gifts to Birdy to seal the bargain, which she initially refuses but later accepts in order to save a bear in a traveling circus. At this point, she fully expects to marry the man. However, at the last minute, Birdy receives word that Shaggy Beard has been killed in a barroom brawl. Instead of him, she is asked to marry his son. Although she feels caged by the customs of her time and is forced to marry this man she does not love, she is relieved that she does not have to marry the father. The novel ends with her acceptance of this fate and her observation that her world is still "full of possibilities."

The book offers an excellent picture of the daily life of those who lived in the Middle Ages. As such, the activities in this section tend to focus on history and daily living. The outline on page 6 is a suggested plan for using the various activities that are presented in this book. Excluding reading time, each activity is designed to take about an hour. The ideas should be adapted to fit your particular classroom and the ability level of your students.

Catherine, Called Birdy

Sample Plan

Lesson 1
- Discuss An Invitation to the Middle Ages. (page 10)
- Read Life for the Nobles and Clergy. (page 11)
- View a section of a movie from the Middle Ages. (See Bibliography, page 78.)

Lesson 2
- Explore a map of medieval Europe. (page 75)
- Read September entries in *Catherine, Called Birdy*.
- Complete Exploration Questions 1 and 2. (page 9)
- Read Life for the Commoners. (page 12)
- Complete Guild Signs. (page 60)
- Introduce and explain Research Project. (page 71)

Lesson 3
- Read October entries in *Catherine, Called Birdy*.
- Complete Exploration Questions 3–5. (page 9)
- Read and discuss Why Were the Jews Expelled from England? (page 14)
- Read and discuss Inside the Castle. (page 15)
- Complete Castle Venn Diagram. (page 16)
- Continue working on a research project.

Lesson 4
- Read November entries in *Catherine, Called Birdy*.
- Complete Exploration Questions 6–8. (page 9)
- Discuss the Comparison Chart. (page 44)
- Assign Create a Limerick. (page 34)
- Continue working on a research project.

Lesson 5
- Read December entries in *Catherine, Called Birdy*.
- Complete Exploration Questions 9 and 10. (page 9)
- Complete Who's in the Castle? (page 13)
- Continue working on a research project.

Lesson 6
- Read January entries in *Catherine, Called Birdy*.
- Complete Exploration Questions 11 and 12. (page 9)
- Read The Story of Last Names. (pages 45 and 46)
- Complete What's in a Name? (page 47)

Lesson 7
- Read February entries in *Catherine, Called Birdy*.
- Read Medieval Clothing and complete the activity. (pages 42 and 43)
- Complete Exploration Questions 13 and 14. (page 9)
- Continue working on a research project.

Lesson 8
- Read March and April entries in *Catherine, Called Birdy*.
- Complete Exploration Questions 15–18. (page 9)
- Assign Making Parchment. (page 56)

Lesson 9
- Read May entries in *Catherine, Called Birdy*.
- Complete Exploration Questions 19 and 20. (page 9)
- Assign Spinner Probability. (pages 35–37)
- Continue working on a research project.

Lesson 10
- Read June entries in *Catherine, Called Birdy*.
- Complete Exploration Questions 21 and 22. (page 9)
- Assign Making a Mural. (page 58)

Lesson 11
- Read July and August entries in *Catherine, Called Birdy*.
- Complete Exploration Questions 23–26. (page 9)
- Present student research projects.
- Assign Stained Glass. (page 59)

Lesson 12
- Finish *Catherine, Called Birdy*.
- Complete Exploration Question 27. (page 9)
- Present student research projects.

Overview of Activities

Setting the Stage

1. Introduce the period of the Middle Ages, using the introductory text on page 10. Make two columns on an overhead or on sheets of butcher paper, labeled "Know" and "Want to Know." Ask students what things they already know about the Middle Ages and what things they want to know. Record these responses. At the end of the unit, add a third column labeled "Learned." Ask students what things they learned from the unit.

2. Several resource pages dealing with daily life and activities during the Middle Ages have been included. These can be read aloud or compiled into a packet to be read by students and used by them as a resource. These sections were designed to provide a historical context for the book and to relate to the book sections for which they are suggested, though they can easily be used independently of them. In some cases, exploration questions have been added to the end of these sections and may be assigned to students.

3. Choose an appropriate video for your class. Several choices are listed in the bibliography on page 78.

4. Prepare a medieval bulletin board. Some ideas and directions can be found on page 73.

Enjoying the Book

1. Assign specific sections for reading each day. Read them as a class or individually, or assign the reading to cooperative groups.

2. Assign a reading time each day for 15–20 minutes.

3. Do Exploration Questions on page 9 as a classroom activity, or have students keep journals of their responses.

4. Discuss the origins and meanings of last names on pages 45 and 46. Have students write their own stories using some of the names.

5. Sponsor a rotating chess and/or checkers tournament. As a more expanded option, you might divide the class in two or involve another class with each player in a group to make only one or two moves for the day.

6. In conjunction with the parchment activity (page 56), you may wish to have students design their own illuminations (page 57).

7. Make a chart comparing life in the Middle Ages with life today. Use the topics on page 44 to get students started. As an extension, ask students what simple items they would most like to take with them if they could go back to the Middle Ages. Which would be most beneficial? Which would be most impressive to the people of that time?

Overview of Activities *(cont.)*

Enjoying the Book *(cont.)*

8. Read Life for the Commoners on page 12. Have students complete the crossword puzzle, Who's in the Castle?, on page 13.

9. Read together Why Were the Jews Expelled from England? on page 14 and have students answer the questions.

10. Read about Medieval Clothing on page 42 and complete the activity on page 43.

11. Have students make shop signs that advertise something they might have sold during the Middle Ages (page 60). Since few people could read or write, shops had to have pictures that clearly advertised what they sold. Have students try to guess what the signs of others represent.

12. Have students draw a map of a medieval manor, labeling all the parts. Remember that a manor had to be self-sufficient, so make sure that each contains the essential elements for living there (e.g., water, food, shelter, shops, agriculture).

13. Use the Venn diagram on page 16 to allow students to explore the ways castles and modern houses are alike and different.

14. Making Ink (page 39) and Keeping Time (page 40) are simple science activities that can be used to interest students in the technology of the Middle Ages.

Extending the Book

1. Play some indoor and outdoor games from the Middle Ages that are suggested on pages 63 and 64.

2. Have students further describe the main characters of the book, using the Character Descriptions activity on page 28 as a guide.

3. Assign students a research project. The topic of this project can be biographical or topical (suggestions are listed on page 71). If you decide to use cooperative groups for this exercise, give each member of the group a distinct responsibility. For instance, one person can be designated the researcher and can be in charge of finding the information that the group will need. A second person can be the recorder and can be responsible for writing down the information that the researcher finds. A third can be the illustrator and draw the pictures and diagrams that the group will need when it presents its topic to the class. Take the time to practice roles.

4. Have students keep diaries of their own lives for two weeks to see what it is like to keep a daily record as Catherine did. Students can note what things they did that day, what they thought about the events of the day, and what new things they learned. As an extension, each student can rewrite one day's entry in *Catherine, Called Birdy* as if he or she were one of the other characters in the scene Birdy describes for that day.

Exploration Questions

Directions: Use these questions created for *Catherine, Called Birdy* to help you keep a journal. Use complete sentences in your answers.

September–November

1. What is the setting (time and place) of the novel?
2. What is Birdy's attitude towards her father? How do you know?
3. What is the attitude in England toward Jews? How do you know?
4. What are some of the jobs that Birdy detests doing around the house?
5. What does Birdy fear will happen between her Uncle George and Aelis?
6. Why can't Birdy take a bath when she develops a rash (November 18)?
7. Summarize the story of how Birdy's father and mother first met. What does Birdy find so strange about the story?
8. Describe the prank that Birdy attempts on November 25. What was the outcome?

December–February

9. How do Birdy's feelings toward hanging change after she actually attends one?
10. Why does Birdy think that Perkin is the luckiest person she knows?
11. On January 11, Birdy makes a list of things that girls are not supposed to do. Which of the items would still be considered impolite today?
12. What hardships are caused by the bad weather at Birdy's manor?
13. What does Birdy's mother mean when she says that having children is like penance?
14. Why does Birdy feel guilty when Aelis wants to talk about George?

March–May

15. From Birdy's description, what do you know about the religious season of Lent?
16. In what way are Agnes and Birdy different? Why does Birdy not like Agnes?
17. What aspects of medieval life do you find surprising so far?
18. Why does Birdy say that she would like to be like Ethelfritha when she gets older?
19. Describe the events of the May Day celebration.
20. When Birdy is fighting with her father, she says that God gave her a big mouth so it should not be a sin to use it. Do you agree with her reasoning? Why or why not?

June–September

21. What "soft feelings" does Birdy feel towards others in her entries throughout June?
22. How is the peddler who sold rotten fish punished? Do you think the punishment was fair?
23. Why does Birdy feel that "men are in charge of making saints"?
24. Brother Norbert and Brother Behrtwald buy saint relics from a soldier. Do you think that the relics are real? Explain your answer.
25. What surprising act does Robert do to help Birdy?
26. What happens during August that shows Birdy's generosity and kindness?
27. Near the end of the novel, Birdy says, "I cannot escape my life but can only use my determination and courage to make it the best I can." How does this statement contrast with Birdy's attitude in the first part of the novel?

An Invitation to the Middle Ages

Return to the days when knights were bold! You are hereby invited to take a journey through the Middle Ages. What was it like then? Who had the power? Get to know the people of that time, but be prepared for surprises. Why was salt so important during the Middle Ages? How could thousands of children set out on a long journey and just disappear? Learn about medieval armor, weapons, and warfare. Bring your curiosity along as you read, write, draw, and play your way back to the age of knights and castles. So, here you go . . .

Two thousand years ago, the Roman Empire was the strongest nation in the world. By 300 A.D., the empire encompassed most of Europe, the northern coast of Africa, Egypt, and parts of the Middle East. The capital city of Rome became a great center of learning, art, government, and trade for those who lived around the Mediterranean Sea. As mighty as it was, with time, Rome became weaker and weaker. Its citizens suffered a series of terrible plagues and droughts. Many animals died, and farmers could not grow as much food as people needed. Some subjects rebelled against harsh rulers, and Rome was less able to defend itself from attack.

At the same time in northern Europe, there lived a savage tribe of people called the *Vandals*. During the fourth and fifth centuries, the Vandals and other tribes attacked the Roman Empire piece by piece. Finally, in 455 A.D., eighty thousand Vandals attacked the city of Rome itself. They burned and looted buildings and even stole the bronze roof off of the capitol building (they thought it was made of gold). Rome was destroyed, and the mighty empire collapsed. For the next 300 years, cities were left in ruins. The vast system of roads crumbled. People had little art or music, and few were taught to read and write. Without strong leaders or laws, gangs of thieves roamed the land, terrorizing the common people. This grim period is called the *Dark Ages*.

But this sad time of the early Middle Ages did not last forever. By the 800s, people began to join together for protection. The warriors who had the most power in each area proclaimed themselves kings. These kings built fortresses or castles in which to live, and people moved around the castles for protection. In return for the protection of the king, peasants farmed the land and paid taxes. The kings in each area appointed followers to be lords of parts of their land. In return for land, each lord promised to pay taxes to the king and help him in battle. This system of society, with the king at the top, the lords in the middle, and the common people at the bottom, became known as the *feudal system*. This type of society proved to be stable for the next thousand years and provides the background for where our story really begins.

Questions

1. Why do you think the city of Rome became such an influence on those who lived around the Mediterranean Sea in terms of learning, art, and government?

2. What would it be like in our society if we had no laws or government?

3. Find out more about the invasion of Rome. Pretend that you are a reporter during this time and write a newspaper account of it.

Life for the Nobles and Clergy

A lord's life centered on fighting. He believed that the only honorable way to live was as a professional warrior. The *lords* and their *knights,* wearing heavy armor and riding huge war horses, fought with lances or swords. In times of peace, a lord and his knights entertained themselves by hunting, practicing for war, and participating in tournaments. When they couldn't go outside, they played dice, checkers, and chess. The lord was also in charge of his manor, resolving disputes and taking care of business. Some lords had several manors and might place a *bailiff* in charge of running the estate while he was away. The lord lived in the manor house or castle.

lady and lord

The lord's wife was called a *lady.* She was trained to sew, spin, weave, and to rule the household servants. Instead of a bailiff, she might take responsibility while the lord was away. Many ladies became excellent businesswomen since their husbands were often gone for long periods of time. The lady was also responsible for receiving and taking care of special guests. Most ladies married early and had little say in the matter. Later on, if a wife did not bear at least one son, the lord could end their marriage! Most lords and ladies did not think that education was necessary, so few could read or write. Although the position of ladies improved as the Middle Ages went on, women still had far fewer rights and opportunities than they do today.

monk

Most *bishops* and other high-ranking priests were noblemen who devoted their lives to the church. Since there was little separation between the church and government, they ruled sections of land and lived much like other noblemen. Some of these clergymen were as wealthy and powerful as the greatest lords. The priest who took care of the castle chapel was called a *chaplain.*

Monks were poorer members of the clergy who lived in monasteries according to strict rules. They had to spend a certain number of hours each day studying, praying, learning about the Bible, and taking part in religious services. At other times, monks organized church services and helped the poor. Many monks were well educated, and monasteries became centers of learning. Some who were outstanding scholars left the monastery and became advisers to kings and other rulers.

Interesting Fact: Many people think that the abbreviation A.D. stands for "After Death" but A.D. actually stands for "Anno Domini," which is Latin for "the year of our Lord." The year "one A.D." is the first year of Jesus Christ's life, not the first year after his death.

Life for the Commoners

Common people, who were also called *villeins,* had few rights and were pretty much at the mercy of the lords. The most important commoner was the *bailiff,* who ran the day-to-day business of the castle. The bailiff was in charge of hiring skilled craftsmen like *masons* to repair the stonework on the castle, *blacksmiths* to make metal weapons and horseshoes, and *fletchers* to make arrows. Some commoners, like laundresses, butlers, and cooks were servants who kept the castle clean and running smoothly. Other castle servants included the *tailor* who mended the lord's clothes, the *groom* who took care of the horses, and the *falconer* who cared for the lord's hunting birds. Some tradespeople who lived in the towns organized *guilds* to help set prices and train new workers. The lowest of the commoners were the *peasants* who farmed the land. With the help of his wife and children, a peasant farmed both the lord's fields and his own. He also performed whatever other tasks the lord demanded, such as cutting wood, storing grain, or repairing roads and bridges.

bailiff

hut

Most peasants lived in crude, one-room huts. The walls of their houses were most often made from *wattle and daub,* woven strips of wood covered by a mixture of cow dung, straw, and mud. Roofs and beds in the cottages were made from straw. Peasants ate black bread, eggs, poultry, and vegetables like cabbage and turnips. Rarely could they afford meat. They could not hunt or fish because game on the manor belonged to the lord. Peasants were considered property of the lord and were bought and sold like animals. (Their children were even called "litters"!) Because of this, they were not allowed to leave the manor except under rare circumstances. Sometimes peasants were able to save up enough money to buy their freedom or gain it by performing some great deed for the lord, but these chances were remote. A final way for the peasant to gain his freedom was this: An ancient law said that a person might gain his or her freedom by escaping from the manor and evading capture for a year and a day. But since food and shelter were scarce and bands of thieves were common, few actually tried this.

Interesting Fact: Peasants lived miserable lives and were looked down on by everyone. Here is what one nobleman wrote about his peasants: "The peasant's head is so hard that no idea can get into it." Another said this: "The devil himself will not take peasants because of their terrible smell."

Who's in the Castle?

Directions: Hidden below are people who hold key jobs in the castle. They can be listed in any direction. The starred words (*) come from the September and October entries in *Catherine, Called Birdy*.

R	E	I	R	R	A	F	B	L	O	R	D	D	O	A	R	F
J	E	W	S	H	A	T	A	X	E	F	P	E	H	E	C	A
B	I	T	B	I	L	D	C	L	W	V	A	S	A	L	X	L
A	F	O	E	E	Y	K	O	O	C	G	G	T	E	I	A	C
G	R	O	O	M	M	P	N	N	E	E	F	Y	S	Q	O
C	H	S	M	E	B	A	O	O	O	N	L	H	A	W	N
H	A	T	R	S	L	R	S	K	M	R	T	E	O	N	F	E
A	R	E	B	S	A	F	O	O	E	G	A	T	R	D	S	R
P	M	W	I	E	U	P	O	I	N	E	I	C	M	P	C	R
L	O	A	L	N	N	Y	N	M	D	J	L	H	A	E	R	T
A	U	R	L	G	D	Z	M	D	K	E	O	E	R	R	I	I
I	R	D	R	E	R	U	S	A	E	R	R	R	S	K	B	A
N	C	A	T	H	E	R	I	N	E	G	U	Y	H	I	E	T
I	R	L	B	C	S	F	F	I	L	I	A	B	A	N	T	O
J	L	L	I	B	S	K	N	I	G	H	T	N	L	J	G	O
S	B	I	S	H	O	P	N	T	N	A	S	A	E	P	B	C

1. mends the lord's clothes
2. takes care of the lord's hunting birds
3. repairs the stonework on the castle
4. is in charge of the castle chapel
5. is in charge of the manor
6. fixes food for the lord and his guests
7. takes care of the horses and stable
8. makes arrows
9. runs the day-to-day business of the castle
10. high-ranking position in the church

11. the lowest class of commoners
12. washes clothes
13. defends the manor
*14. Birdy's real name
*15. Birdy's two best friends   .
*16. one task Birdy detests
*17. people who must leave England
*18. Edward's job
*19. Birdy's uncle
20. the lord's wife

Why Were the Jews Expelled from England?

Birdy's journal for October 3 talks about a group of Jewish travelers who are fleeing the country. Birdy's mother takes pity on the travelers and allows them to stay overnight. Birdy makes the comment that the Jews must leave England by order of the king, who has decreed that Jews are wicked and dangerous. What's going on here?

During the Middle Ages, two groups controlled the opinions of most people—the Christian Church and the lords. Local rulers generally welcomed Jews because they were good business people, and they would lend money when the church refused. This made Jews excellent sources of tax money, so most lords protected them. On the other hand, because Jews and Christians disagreed about religious matters, the Church discouraged its members from doing business with Jews.

During the latter part of the Middle Ages, Christians began to take over the roles of bankers for the lords. Kings began to demand higher and higher taxes from the Jews, which made it difficult for them to continue to lend money. Since many people still owed money to the Jews, some began to harass them and spread rumors about them in hopes that the Jews would leave and forget about the money owed to them. Finally, in 1290, King Edward issued an edict expelling all of the Jews from England. The Jewish people were allowed to take only their personal possessions, and all other property was seized by the king. In addition, all debts owed to them were cancelled. During that year, about 4,000 Jews were forced to leave England, and other European countries issued similar decrees in following years.

Directions: Use this page and the information in *Catherine, Called Birdy* to help you answer the questions below.

1. Why do you think the Jews were resented in the Middle Ages?

   _____

   _____

2. In what way does the scene with Birdy and the Jewish travelers comment on the banishment of the Jews from England?

   _____

   _____

3. How do you think the author feels about this event?

   _____

   _____

4. What would you have done as king during this time?

   _____

   _____

Inside the Castle

From the outside, castles may have looked impressive, but on the inside they were mostly dark, cold, and drafty. Tapestries were hung on the wall to help brighten up the halls and keep in the heat. The main furniture in the *great hall* were wooden benches and large tables made by laying wood planks across other benches. At night, the table was taken down to make room for the servants who slept on the floor. The floors were covered year-round with reeds, bones, and scraps of food. When the room began to smell, the servants added more reeds and sprinkled spices to help fight the odor. Once a year, the servants replaced the soiled reeds with new ones, and the whole process started again. The king and his family often shared a single room where their sleeping quarters were separated only by curtains.

The king's kitchen staff decorated most of the food before they served it. Sometimes when meat was served, the servants put the fur or feathers back on the meat to make it look alive! On the other hand, because there was no refrigeration, the food spoiled quickly. Sometimes when food was spoiled, they just dumped extra gravy on it and served it anyway. One of the only ways to preserve and season food was to salt all the meat. In fact, since salt was so important at the medieval table, it began to be a sort of status symbol. Most great halls only had one large salt container, and where you sat in relation to it told people how important you were. The more important people sat "above the salt," and those who were less important sat "below the salt." During evening meals, the lord and his family sat upon a raised platform called a *dais* and watched *court jesters* who sang, juggled, and told a few tales. Fireplaces, torches, and candles had to be used to light the dark rooms even during the daytime.

Castles had no modern plumbing, but garbage disposal presented no problem. The servants dumped it in the moat! Bathrooms in castles, which were called *garderobes,* often emptied right into the moat as well. Since people in the Middle Ages believed that washing too much could make you sick, bathing became a once-a-month affair. Most didn't even bother with soap, mainly used it for washing clothes. In fact, soap in those days was so strong it could eat holes through cloth, and since the royal family preferred dirt to holes, wash days were few and far between.

Interesting Fact: The superstitious people of the Middle Ages believed that there were "sprites" that were always trying to cause trouble for people. Telling a person to "break a leg" before an important event was one way to throw these spirits off and make something good happen instead. Another way they believed to throw them off was to knock on wood after something good was said. The sound of knocking would cover your words and the "sprites" would leave you alone.

Castle Venn Diagram

Directions: Use the pattern below to think of the ways that castles and houses are alike and different. In the areas where the boxes intersect, write the things that Middle Ages castles and modern houses have in common. In the other parts, write the things that make them different.

castles

both

houses

Proud Taste for Scarlet and Miniver

by E. L. Konigsburg

(Bantam Doubleday Dell Books for Young Readers, 1973)

Summary

This is the story of Eleanor of Aquitaine, told as if she and three close friends are waiting in heaven for judgment to be passed on her second husband. As a young woman, she is married to Louis VII, who immediately inherits the throne of France. When Louis has a religious conversion several years later, the two begin to disagree about how they should live. Eleanor is accustomed to luxury and with her husband's newfound piety, the conflict sets off a series of disagreements that ends their marriage. She quickly marries Henry II, and the two have sons who vie for the thrones of northern France and England. Eleanor schemes to ensure that her sons are placed on the throne.

Sample Plan

Lesson 1

- Explore the map of medieval England and France. (page 75)
- View first segment of the video *Castle* and discuss.
- Complete Making of a Knight. (pages 48 and 49)

Lesson 2

- Introduce *Proud Taste for Scarlet and Miniver*.
- Discuss points of view and four main characters.
- Read Part 1, Chapters 1–3.
- Complete Exploration Questions 1–3. (page 20)
- View second segment of the video *Castle* and discuss.
- Read Outside the Castle. (pages 21 and 22)

Lesson 3

- Read Part 1, Chapters 4–7.
- Complete Exploration Questions 4–6. (page 20)
- View third segment of the video *Castle* and discuss.
- Complete Castle for Sale. (page 23)
- Introduce culminating activities. (pages 67–72)

Lesson 4

- Read Part 1, Chapters 8–10.
- Complete Exploration Questions 7 and 8. (page 20)
- View fourth segment of the video *Castle* and discuss.
- Complete Coat of Arms. (pages 24 and 25)
- Continue culminating activities.

Lesson 5

- Read Part 2, Chapters 1–4.
- Complete Exploration Questions 9 and 10. (page 20)
- Complete Catapults activity. (page 41)

Lesson 6

- Read Part 2, Chapters 5–8.
- Complete Exploration Questions 11–13. (page 20)
- Read The Feudal System and discuss. (pages 54 and 55)
- Complete Castle Cross. (page 26)

- Continue culminating activities.

Lesson 7

- Read Part 2, Chapters 9–12.
- Complete Exploration Questions 14 and 15. (page 20)
- Read The Crusades and complete Crusader Quest activity. (pages 52 and 53)
- Continue culminating activities.
- Play The Game of Piggy. (page 38)

Lesson 8

- Read Part 3, Chapters 1–5.
- Complete Exploration Questions 16–18. (page 20)
- Complete Medieval Word Scramble. (page 33)
- Continue culminating activities.

Lesson 9

- Read Part 3, Chapters 6–11.
- Complete Exploration Questions 19 and 20. (page 20)
- Complete Design Your Own Coin. (page 62)
- Continue culminating activities.

Lesson 10

- Read Part 4, Chapters 1–2.
- Complete Exploration Questions 21–23. (page 20)
- Read The Death of the Middle Ages and discuss. (page 65)
- Distribute Medieval Post Test. (page 66)
- Continue culminating activities.

Lesson 11

- Finish Part 4.
- Complete Exploration Question 24. (page 20)
- Complete Eleanor's Character Web. (page 27)
- View a movie on the Middle Ages. (See Bibliography, page 78.)

Lesson 12

- Complete Point of View. (page 29)
- Continue culminating activities.

Overview of Activities

Setting the Stage

1. Use David Macaulay's *Castle* video (listed in the bibliography on page 78) as an introduction to castles and medieval life. There are two versions of this video, and the one you will want is broken into four 15-minute sections. This version also includes a study guide with discussion questions and vocabulary words.

2. Several resource pages dealing with castles, the Crusades, and other historical events during the Middle Ages have been included. These can be read aloud or compiled into a packet to be read by students and used by them as a resource. These sections were designed to provide a historical context for the book and to relate to the book sections for which they are suggested, though they can easily be used independently of them. In some cases, exploration questions have been added to the ends of these sections and may be assigned to students. If *Proud Taste for Scarlet and Miniver* is read without first having read *Catherine, Called Birdy*, you may want to consider including some of the previous sections (e.g., Life for the Nobles and Clergy on page 11, Life for the Commoners on page 12, Inside the Castle on page 15) as reading assignments to give students a background on life in the Middle Ages.

3. Choose an appropriate video for your class. Several choices are listed in the bibliography on page 78.

4. Introduce the historical characters of King Henry II, Eleanor of Aquitaine, and their sons Henry, Richard the Lion-Hearted, Geoffrey, and John Lackland. Refer to the bibliography for sources of information about these and other characters.

5. Display maps of medieval England and France. Locate principal cities and point out places important to the story. Refer to the maps throughout the medieval unit. Compare these to a modern map of Europe and discuss the boundary and name changes.

6. Construct a bulletin board tracing the routes of Eleanor and Louis on their Crusade. Record Eleanor's reaction to the different cities.

7. Have students draw life-size figures to represent each of the four storytellers in the book.

Enjoying the Book

1. Assign specific sections to be read each day. Read the book as a class or individually, or assign the reading to cooperative groups.

2. Assign a reading time each day for 15–20 minutes.

3. Do the Exploration Questions on page 20 as a classroom activity or have students keep a journal of their responses.

4. Prior to reading the section on Armor (pages 50 and 51), brainstorm the kinds of protective suits that are worn today (e.g., football pads, bike helmet, bullet-proof vest). Have students design a suit of armor incorporating what they know.

5. Have students design castles on paper as if they were medieval real estate agents (page 23).

Overview of Activities *(cont.)*

Enjoying the Book *(cont.)*

6. Read Outside the Castle with students and answer questions (pages 21–22).

7. Each student can create a personal coat of arms that tells others what he or she is like on page 25. Students can use page 24 to assist them in choosing colors, symbols, and their correct marks of cadency.

8. After reading Catapults on page 41, have students work in groups to design a model catapult as shown. Take students outside for a throwing contest and then allow them to revise their catapults. Which shoots farthest? Which is most accurate? As an alternative, this project can be assigned as homework, to be tested on the last day.

9. Compare and contrast several of the Crusades. What were the important dates and people associated with each? What were their purposes? Where did they start and end up? On a bulletin board, map the routes that the crusaders took toward the Holy Land.

10. Discuss the role of money and complete the Design Your Own Coin activity on page 62.

11. Explore the characteristics of Eleanor of Aquitaine, using the character web found on page 27. A character web is a writing technique that is used to break down and examine the traits of a character. The center of the web contains the name of the character. The second layer contains traits that describe the character. The third layer gives events from the story to support the traits.

12. Have students choose four of the characters and four adjectives to describe each one (page 28). Have students write a sentence about each character using the adjective.

13. Have students write a story from the point of view of one the characters (page 29). As an option, use the scroll on page 74 to write the story.

Extending the Book

1. Play some indoor and outdoor games from the Middle Ages that are suggested on pages 63 and 64.

2. Sample the recipes listed on pages 68–70 as part of classtime or as preparation for a Medieval Festival.

3. Organize a Medieval Festival, using the suggestions on page 67. Students can be assigned roles for this event (e.g., peasants, servers, entertainers, king, queen) and work on their projects during class. Use the invitations provided on page 76 to invite parents and relatives to the festival.

4. Read the "Pardoner's Tale" (pages 30 and 31) and discuss the role of storytelling in the Middle Ages. Students can write their own short stories, using a starter idea on page 32.

5. Use Medieval Word Scramble (page 33) and Castle Cross (page 26) as a review of basic medieval terms used in the unit.

Exploration Questions

Directions: Use these questions to help you keep a journal. Use complete sentences in your answers.

Part 1

1. Who are the four main characters in the first scene? What is your initial impression of each?
2. What are some of Louis' fears about Eleanor before he meets her?
3. What does Abbot Suger find so striking about the prayer of Eleanor's father?
4. Why does Abbot Suger say that it is okay for Louis to come inside the church even though he has been excommunicated?
5. What reason does Abbot Bernard give for why he believes that Eleanor and Louis' marriage is not valid in God's eyes?
6. What are some of the ways in which Louis and Eleanor travel differently on their crusade?
7. What were some of the things that made it difficult for the crusaders to travel quickly and easily? What would you have done to speed them up?
8. In Antioch, the crusaders meet Eleanor's cousin Raymond. In what ways is he more like Eleanor than Louis?

Part 2

9. What is the "Truce of God"? Why do you think this might have encouraged people to go on a crusade?
10. What changes does Eleanor make to her castle after she marries Henry?
11. Why were the English people so impressed with the way that Henry and Eleanor arrived in England?
12. List the names and birth order of Henry and Eleanor's children.
13. How did Henry change the court system of England? What else would you have changed?
14. Henry would like to make Thomas Becket the Archbishop of Canterbury. Why does Matilda think this would be a bad idea?
15. What is meant by the phrase "neck verses"?

Part 3

16. What were the two reasons Eleanor went to Aquitaine?
17. What were the "Courts of Love"? Why were they formed?
18. Why was John called "Lackland"? What did Henry intend to do about it?
19. What were some of the ways that Eleanor had the ancient stories of Arthur and his knights changed? Why do you think she did this?
20. How do you know that young Henry has a change of heart before he dies?

Part 4

21. Why does Eleanor say that she chose to be 67 in heaven?
22. What are some of the things Eleanor did to make Richard a famous king?
23. How does Eleanor strike a deal with the merchants of the towns?
24. What was the "Magna Carta"? Why was John forced to sign it?

Outside the Castle

The first castles looked a lot like early American forts. First, a large ditch, or *moat,* was dug, and the dirt from it was used to make a giant mound in the middle. At the top of this mound, a fence of sharpened wooden stakes, called a *palisade,* was built with a wooden tower in the middle. This tower, sometimes called a *keep,* was the strongest and most secure part of the castle. The lord could live here and fight if the enemy ever got close. The keep could only be reached by climbing up a tall ladder, which was pulled up in times of war. Another fenced area surrounding the mound was called a *bailey* and held other castle buildings like stables, storerooms, and a chapel. Every castle also had its own well. These early wooden castles were better than nothing, but you can probably imagine what their main weakness was. Attackers often burned the castles to the ground!

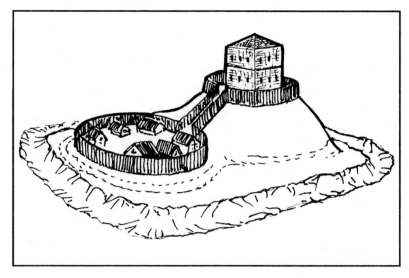

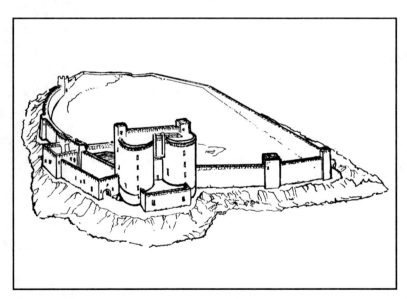

Because of the fire danger, lords began to do away with wooden palisades during the 900s. They were replaced by sturdier stone walls that did not burn. Straw and wooden roofs were replaced by a thin type of rock called *slate.* Some lords also built towers around their castles and added *battlements* to the tops of the walls and towers. Battlements had low places called *crenels* where archers could look and shoot through and high parts called *merlons* where they could hide when under attack. Towers in a castle were well stocked with food and supplies and, in the event of an attack, could be closed off and independently defended. Castles built later had other advances, like *arrow loops* where archers could fire arrows at attackers and still be protected. Despite all these advances, the idea of the castle was still to protect the lord, his family, and followers and to provide a base for the community.

Rebel tribes like the Welsh were always a problem, so a king often had several castles that controlled different parts of his land. Since he could not be in charge of all of them at once, he gave some of them to people he could trust. In return, these lords gave the king their loyalty and provided him with knights to fight his battles.

Outside the Castle *(cont.)*

To *breach,* or gain entrance to, a castle was a difficult and costly task. A moat was the first obstacle that attackers faced in trying to lay *siege* to a castle. Since castles didn't have any real plumbing, most moats were filled with sewage and human waste. A moat that was full of sewage meant that attacking armies would have trouble getting large weapons close to the castle and wouldn't want to camp near it. Other moats that were dry had sharpened sticks in the ground to slow attacking soldiers.

Most moats had a drawbridge that could be pulled up in times of attack. A heavy *portcullis*, a metal gate that sealed off the front entrance, gave extra protection. Attackers who got close or broke through the portcullis often had boiling oil or water poured on them from *murder holes* cut into the walls and ceiling above. If attackers used ladders to try to climb inside, they risked being pushed away with poles or having stones dropped on their heads.

Instead of attacking the castle directly, many attackers dug tunnels instead. Protected from arrows by strong wooden roofs, some armies tried to dig straight under the wall and into the castle courtyard. Wooden logs held the tunnels up while the men worked. More often, however, they simply burned the wooden supports in the tunnel just before it was completed in hopes that the ground and wall over it would collapse.

The final way to gain entrance to a castle was simply to wait. Attackers cut off escape from the castle in hopes that those inside would run out of food and be forced to surrender.

Questions

1. In a dictionary, find these words: *fort, palisade, bailey, defense, portcullis, tapestry, breach,* and *stalemate.* Use each of the words in a sentence.

2. There are many similarities between palisade castles and early American forts. Draw a picture of them both and label some of the ways the two were similar and different.

3. Find out more about the Welsh and the Scottish. Why were they such a problem for the English? In what ways were these people like the natives of North America?

4. Transform your classroom into a castle! Rearrange desks, and use construction paper and rolls of colored paper to create a drawbridge, moat, bailey, keep, and dungeon. Remember to make a flag to tell others about your kingdom.

Castle for Sale

Directions: Pretend that you are trying to sell a castle, and write a real estate ad for it. Draw both a floor plan and a front view. Make sure to note any special features that might appeal to buyers.

For Sale!

(picture)

Special Features: _____

_____

Location: _____

_____

Protection and Defense: _____

_____

Living Quarters: _____

_____

Price: _____

Coat of Arms

When knights began to wear armor, they soon discovered that during wars and tournaments they couldn't tell one another apart. Since very few of them could read, each chose a symbol to be painted onto his shield. A knight might also have had this symbol sewn onto the coat he wore over his armor. This was called a *coat of arms*. Some knights chose people, animals, monsters, and other objects. Others chose an event in the knight's life or some outstanding quality. Some countries used designs on the shields to indicate family relationships. For instance, in Great Britain, *marks of cadency* were used to distinguish one son's coat of arms from another.

Directions: Use this page to help you design a shield of your own on page 25, using the symbols, sports, and hobbies in which you are interested. Follow the steps below to help you make your coat of arms.

1. Decide what colors you will use. The colors should tell about what kind of person you are. Here are the meanings of some colors:

   - gold—generosity
   - red—brave and strong; a warrior's color
   - green—hope and joy; a nature color

   - blue—loyalty and truth
   - purple—royalty
   - black—grief or steadfastness

2. Choose symbols that tell about you. Some of them can be traditional symbols from the Middle Ages. Other symbols can tell about what kind of hobbies you have or what you like to do with your time. Here are some symbols that you might want to use:

   - battleax or other weapon—strength in battle
   - falcon, eagle, or other bird—strength, bravery, or freedom
   - arrowhead—speed and stability; readiness for battle
   - plant, flower, or tree—life and nature
   - shovel, hammer, or other tool—hard work

   - tower—strength and protection
   - unicorn—purity and freedom of spirit
   - dragon—protection
   - deer—peace and harmony
   - lightning bolt—swiftness and power
   - sword—justice and honor

3. Choose the mark of cadency that tells the order in which you were born in your family.

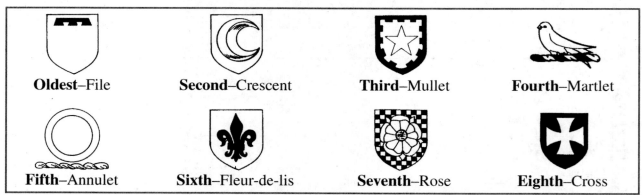

Oldest–File	**Second**–Crescent	**Third**–Mullet	**Fourth**–Martlet
Fifth–Annulet	**Sixth**–Fleur-de-lis	**Seventh**–Rose	**Eighth**–Cross

4. After you have designed your shield on the following page, cut it out and glue it to colored construction paper.

Coat of Arms *(cont.)*

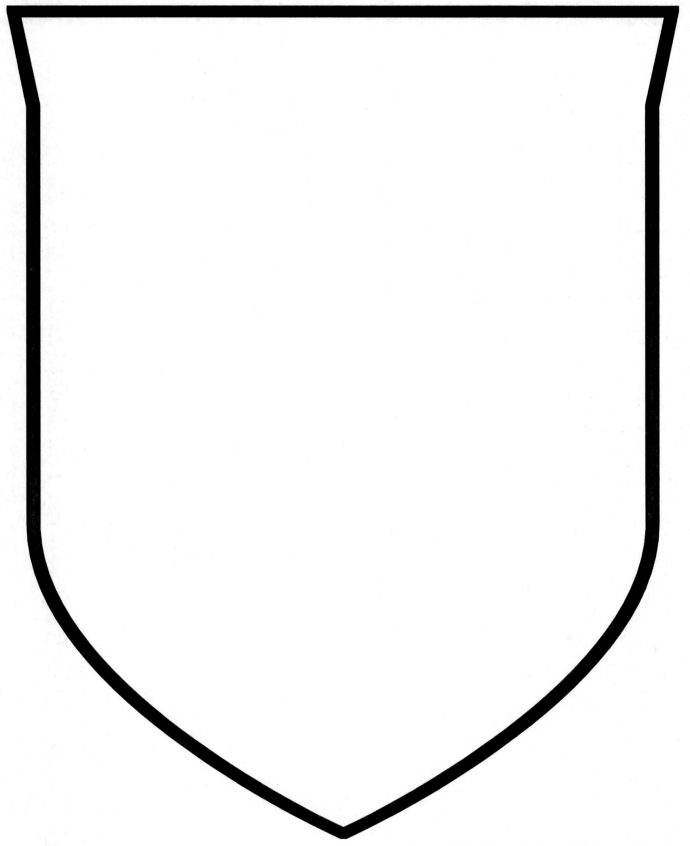

Castle Cross

Directions: Use your knowledge of the Middle Ages and the clues below to complete the crossword. The starred words (*) come from the book *Proud Taste for Scarlet and Miniver*.

Across

1. draw_____
*3. John's nickname
*6. "City of Lights"
9. _____ Loops
10. high places to hide behind and low places to shoot through
12. court for heretics
14. rebel tribe; enemy of the English
16. opposite of offense
*17. Eleanor organized the Courts of _____

Down

1. goal of a siege
2. central meeting and dining area
*4. beautiful city in the East
*5. Henry and Eleanor's second son
*7. eight journeys to the Holy Lands
8. not chain but _____ armor
*11. Thomas _____
13. castle roof material
15. most secure part of the castle

Eleanor's Character Web

Directions: A character web is a writing technique that is used to break down and illustrate the traits of a character. The center of the web contains the name of the character. The second layer contains traits that describe the character. The third layer gives events from the story to support the traits. Explore the characteristics of Eleanor of Aquitaine, using the character web. Create your web on a large piece of paper and use the model below to help you.

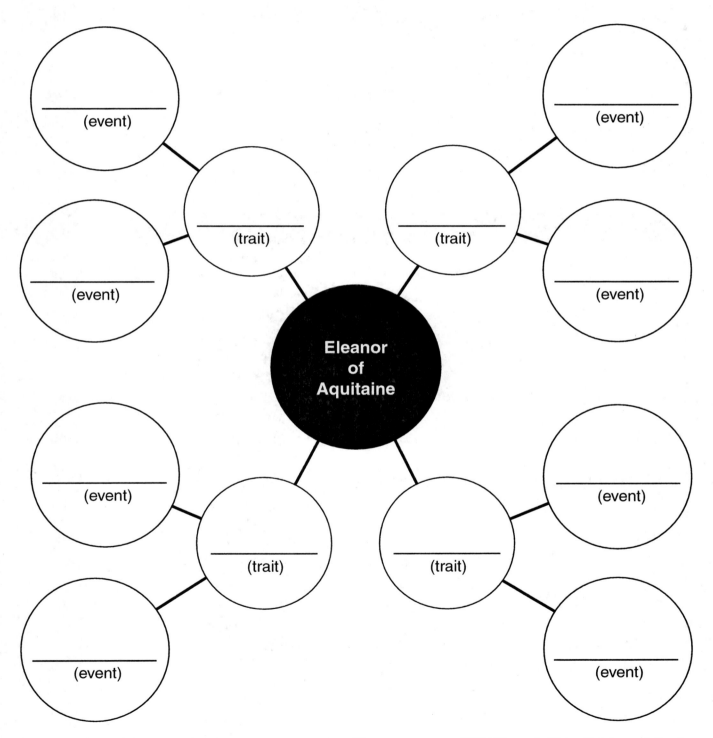

Character Descriptions

Directions: An adjective is a word that describes a person, place, or thing. Choose four of the characters from the book *Proud Taste for Scarlet and Miniver* and four adjectives to describe each one. Use each adjective in a sentence about the person. Use a separate piece of paper for your answer.

Characters		
Queen Eleanor	King Henry	John
Abbot Suger	King Louis	Thomas Becket
William the Marshall	Richard	Matilda

Adjectives			
ambitious	elaborate	jealous	protecting
arrogant	excited	joyful	proud
bold	expert	keen	quiet
brave	friendly	lazy	reckless
charming	generous	leader	responsible
clever	greedy	loving	sad
conceited	humble	pious	smart
demanding	humorous	plain	strong
disagreeable	independent	popular	tireless
devoted	intelligent	proper	wild

Point of View

Proud Taste for Scarlet and Miniver is told from the point of view of four characters. Because each character has a different personality, each tells his or her version of the story slightly differently. For instance, Eleanor and King Louis disagree about how they should present themselves. Eleanor believes that since most common people never get a chance to see nice things, people's lives were made better by seeing her lavish clothing and jewelry. On the other hand, King Louis believes the duty of a king is to live a simple and plain life and to set an example for the commoners.

Directions: Follow the steps below to write a story from a different point of view.

1. Find a group of students who are interested in the same character as you. The following is a list of possible characters:

Queen Eleanor	King Henry	John
Abbot Suger	King Louis	Thomas Becket
William the Marshall	Richard	Matilda

2. Choose a major event from the story and brainstorm how this character might have described it differently from the book.

3. Write the story. Make sure to include your character's observations about the person who actually told the story, as well as any other important information.

4. Add artwork and a title page to the story.

5. Share the story with another group.

Tales of the Times

A favorite pastime during the Middle Ages was storytelling. Travelers were often invited to a lord's table to tell stories of the things they had seen in their travels. Some traveling storytellers became rich! For example, while on a pilgrimage in 1386, Geoffrey Chaucer wrote down several of the tales he heard from fellow travelers. His book, *The Canterbury Tales,* is one of the most famous of the Middle Ages. This is a retelling of one of these stories, the "Pardoner's Tale."

Directions: Read the story, "Pardoner's Tale" from *The Canterbury Tales* by Geoffrey Chaucer, and then complete the activity on page 32.

Pardoner's Tale

In Flanders, there lived three scoundrels who did nothing but gamble and drink and swear. One day as they were sitting in a tavern drinking, they saw a corpse being dragged past on the way to be buried. When they asked the barkeep who the man was, he replied, "Don't you know? Last night while this poor man was drunk out of his mind, the thief whom people call Death crept up behind him, pulled his heart out, and left without saying a word!"

At hearing this, the three began to laugh and curse and call the barkeep a liar. "No masters, I swear it is true!" said the barkeep. "Death has killed thousands in these parts. Men, women, children . . . . It is even said that he lives near here. Dear masters, if I were you, I'd steer clear of this enemy."

"Ha!" cried one of the men, "I'd love to meet the old bugger. I'd show him a thing or two!" He turned to his friends. "Listen you two, let's make a pact to slay this rascal, Death. By God's bones, he who has killed so many will himself be killed before tonight!" So, having nothing better to do and being more than a little bit drunk, the three set off.

They hadn't gone more than half a mile when they met an old man wrapped in a cloak. One of the rogues taunted the old man. "Where do you think you're going, you ugly pile of bones? And how do you come to be so old in spite of this fellow, Death?"

The old man looked straight at him and said, "It is not right for you to taunt a poor old man. Death has placed a curse on me. I walk along like a prisoner in this old body, begging Death to let me die. But he won't even do me that favor! So you see, my years of following after Death have left me withered and gray. Oh, masters, Death has gotten the best of me too. Now let me go."

Another of the three knocked the old man down, "Not so fast, you old dog. Tell us where that fool, Death, has gone, or we'll beat it out of you."

Tales of the Times *(cont.)*

"Dear sirs," the old man replied, "if you're so eager to find Death, just follow this crooked road up the hill. I left him in a grove of trees under a large oak. But I hope you know what you're doing."

"We are far more clever than you, old man," one of the men declared. And with that, the three rascals ran up the hill to the tree of which the old man had spoken. Under the tree they found eight sacks of gold, and Death was nowhere to be seen. "I told you that Death was nobody to be afraid of," one of these men told the other two. "Death is too afraid to show his ugly face and left this bribe here instead!"

The worst of the men spoke up. "My brothers, with this money, each of us can live like kings for the rest of our lives. As soon as it's dark, let's carry the money away to one of our homes." He pointed towards the youngest one. "Why don't you take a couple of these coins into town and get us some bread and wine. We two will stay here and guard the treasure until you get back."

The youngest had just set off for town when a smile crept over the face of the worst. He said to the middle one, "Friend, there certainly is enough gold for all three of us to live on, but honestly I'm not sure that this other fellow is worthy of it. What would you say to keeping all the gold for ourselves?"

"Go on," said the other slowly, "I'm listening."

"Well then," said the worst, "When that other fellow comes back, what do you say that I distract him while you stick your knife in him?" And so, these two agreed to murder the third.

On his way to town, the youngest was feeling the shiny gold coins in his pocket. He began to think, "Why should I have to share my treasure with those two idiots? What did they ever do for me? If only there was a way to get the whole treasure to myself . . . ." And as he walked toward town, a smile began to form on his face.

When he got into town, he hurried to the chemist and bought a large box of rat poison. With the remaining money, he went next door and purchased a loaf of bread and three bottles of wine. Into two of these bottles he emptied the poison, but the third he left alone. On his way back to his companions, he organized a plan to carry all the gold back to town by himself.

And so you can guess how this tale ends. When the youngest arrived with the food, he was murdered by the other two. When the deed was done, the men said, "Now let's drink up and congratulate ourselves on our cleverness." And so the three clever scoundrels met Death after all.

Your Own Robin Hood Story

Directions: Tales like the "Pardoner's Tale" in *The Canterbury Tales* by Geoffrey Chaucer were popular during the Middle Ages. Use this story starter to help you begin your own story about another popular character, Robin Hood.

_____

(title)

by _____

(name)

Although Robin and his men were unaware of it, the Sheriff of Nottingham was closing in on them. By the light of the full moon, the Sheriff crept toward the sleeping men. _____

_____

_____

_____

_____

_____

_____

_____

_____

_____

_____

_____

_____

_____

Medieval Word Scramble

Directions: Work in a group to unscramble the following words from the Middle Ages. Use the boxed letters to solve the bonus words.

1. SAID ___ ___ □ ___

2. SOUJT ___ ___ □ ___ ___

3. EDAPSILA ___ ___ ___ ___ ___ □ ___ ___

4. ALIM ___ ___ ___ □

5. ARETG LAHL □ ___ ___ ___ ___   ___ ___ ___

BONUS WORD: A Middle Ages craftsman might have belonged to a ___ ___ ___ ___ ___

6. IMPWEL ___ ___ □ ___ ___ ___

7. EMARNUTTON ___ □ ___ ___ ___ ___ ___ ___ ___

8. FAILIFB ___ □ ___ ___ ___ ___ ___

9. LCROULTPIS ___ ___ ___ □ ___ ___ ___ ___ ___

BONUS WORD: The best place to put castle trash was the ___ ___ ___ ___ .

10. PEKE ___ ___ □ ___

11. RESTJE ___ ___ ___ □ ___ ___

12. TNETLMABTE ___ □ ___ ___ ___ ___ ___ ___ ___

13. CEELNRS ___ ___ ___ ___ ___ □ ___

14. ACPLTTAU ___ ___ ___ ___ ___ □ ___

BONUS WORD: Roofs were often made out of ___ ___ ___ ___ ___ .

15. AMNRO □ □ ___ ___ ___

16. HCAVYILR □ ___ □ ___ ___ ___ ___

17. IVLINLE ___ □ ___ □ ___ ___ □ ___

18. HCAPLE ___ □ ___ ___ ___ ___

19. RDROEAGEB ___ □ ___ ___ ___ ___ ___ ___

BONUS WORDS: Probably too heavy to send in the mail:___ ___ ___ ___ ___

___ ___ ___ ___

Create a Limerick

A *limerick* is a nonsense poem that was popular during the Middle Ages. Limericks are made up of five lines. Lines one, two, and five rhyme (3 sets of 2 unaccented syllables followed by 1 accented) and lines three and four rhyme (2 sets of 2 unaccented syllables followed by 1 accented). Here are two examples:

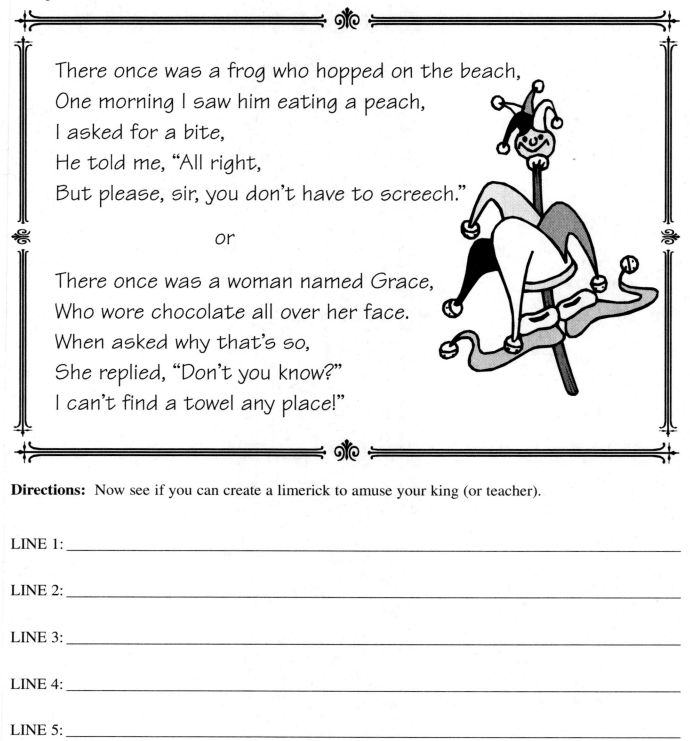

There once was a frog who hopped on the beach,
One morning I saw him eating a peach,
I asked for a bite,
He told me, "All right,
But please, sir, you don't have to screech."

or

There once was a woman named Grace,
Who wore chocolate all over her face.
When asked why that's so,
She replied, "Don't you know?"
I can't find a towel any place!"

Directions: Now see if you can create a limerick to amuse your king (or teacher).

LINE 1: _____

LINE 2: _____

LINE 3: _____

LINE 4: _____

LINE 5: _____

Spinner Probability

During the Middle Ages, probability games like dice, cards, and gambling were popular. The concept of probability in which one situation is more likely than another was very important to know. This activity provides experience collecting and interpreting data. Children can work in cooperative groups. Each child will need a spinner and a die.

Materials

- two spinner tops
- Spinner Recording Sheet (page 36)
- large paper clips
- plastic straws
- scissors
- tape
- 5" x 8" (13 cm x 20 cm) index cards
- paper for recording

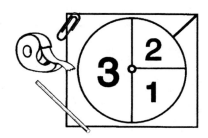

Directions for Spinner

1. Duplicate the two types of spinner tops on page 37 onto cardstock, and have students cut them out. (It's important that they are cut out carefully so that the spinner will spin accurately.)

2. Cut one end off the index cards so the cards are approximately 5" (13 cm) square. Unfold one arm of the paper clip so that the clip lays flat on the desk with the one arm pointed upwards.

3. Make a dot in the approximate middle of the card and draw a line from the dot to one of the corners. Poke the paper clip through the center dot and tape the clip to the bottom of the card. Lay the card and clip on the desk.

4. Cut approximately ¹/₄" (.6 cm) off the straw. Slip the straw piece down the upturned arm of the paper clip followed by the spinner top. Cover the tip of the upturned paper clip with a piece of tape. The spinner should now be able to spin the top. The experiment is designed for the spinner face with the large 3, but if desired, the experiment can be repeated with the second (equally divided) spinner top.

Directions for Spinner Recording Sheet

1. Use the Spinner Recording Sheet on page 36 to keep track of how many times each of the numbers comes up. Before you try it out, answer the following questions in a group: Describe the top of the spinner. What does it look like? When you spin the spinner, which number will have the best chance of coming up? Why do you think so?

2. Write the numbers 1, 2, and 3 in the bottom squares on the Spinner Recording Sheet. Now, keep a record of what number comes up when you spin the spinner. When one number comes up, put an X in the box over that number. Stop your experiment when one column gets to the top of the sheet.

3. Use another sheet and run the experiment again. Do the experiment a total of three times.

4. Now cut out the Xs for each column and tape them together to see how they compare. Get all the columns for your whole class and tape them together. Any differences?

5. Now draw a picture of the spinner and describe the experiment. Write down your answers to these questions: How do the number of 1s and 2s compare? How do these compare to the number of 3s? How did this fit your prediction at the beginning of the experiment? If the number areas had been all the same size on the spinner top, how would your outcome have been different?

Spinner Probability *(cont.)*

Spinner Recording Sheet

Spinner Probability *(cont.)*

Spinner Faces #1

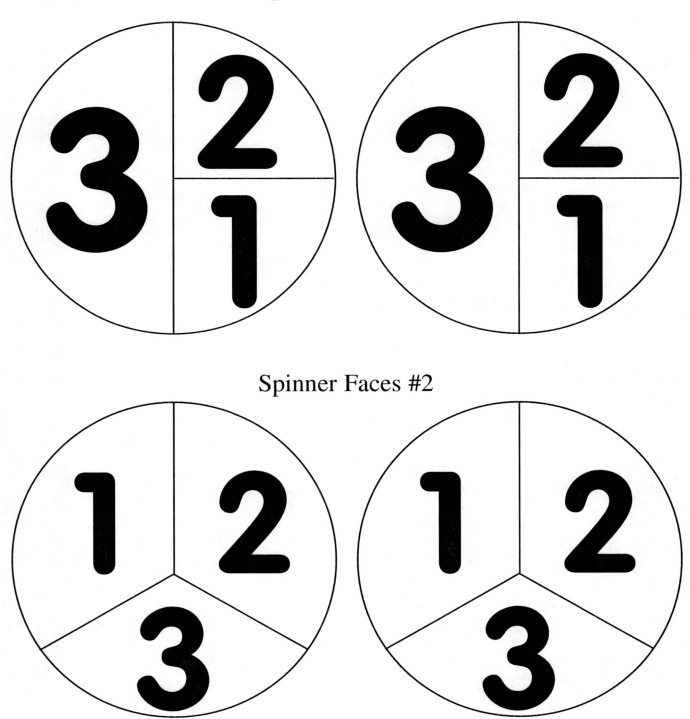

Spinner Faces #2

The Game of Piggy

Piggy is a probability and adding game with dice. Children can play in small groups, or the class as a whole can participate.

Materials

- dice (one pair per student group)
- recording paper and pencil

Directions

1. One player is designated as the "roller" and has the job of rolling the dice until the game is won. The others are "players" and play the game. Players record and keep a running total of the numbers rolled by the two dice.

2. The goal for the players is to be the first to get a score of 101 or more. Players can choose to stop at any time and circle the number of points they have accumulated.

3. If a seven comes up, any player who has not stopped loses all the points he or she has accumulated. At the next roll, all players start again.

4. When one player reaches 101, he or she wins the round and becomes the next roller.

Players	Roll Scores								
	1	2	3	4	5	6	7	8	9
A	6	11 ^17	4 ^21						
B	8	10 ^18	2 ^20						
C	5	5							
D									
E									

Extensions

- To extend the game, have students record their strategy for winning. (For example: Do you stick with smaller numbers, or do you risk your points by going for higher ones? How did your strategy change as you played?)

- Students give their estimates for rolling different numbers on one die. Have children keep a record while another rolls numbers from a single die. After establishing that, over the long run, all numbers are equally likely, discuss the likelihood of rolling a particular number.

Making Ink

Very Berry Ink

Materials

- ripe blueberries or strawberries
- small jars with lids
- spoons
- water
- eyedropper (optional)
- calligraphy pens
- paper towels
- paper cups

Directions

1. Remove stems and leaves from ripe berries. Place berries in a small jar. Mixing different kinds of berries will produce different-colored inks.

2. Press the berries to a pulp with the back of a spoon.

3. When the berries are crushed, add a little water. Add water by the eyedropper or a teaspoon, one drop at a time. The more water you add, the lighter the color of ink.

4. Stir the mixture well.

5. Place a sheet of paper towel over a paper cup. Push the paper towel down into the cup.

6. Slowly pour the berry mixture through the towel into the cup.

7. Let all of the liquid drain through the towel. This is the slow part of the process. Remove the towel and throw it away.

8. Pour the strained ink back into the jar. Use the jar as an ink container.

9. Calligraphy pens come in various sizes. A straight pen has a pointed nib and is most like a fountain pen. Experiment with different pen points and shapes. These pens are available at most art and stationery stores.

10. This ink can be used to write letters or copy student-written poems.

Reappearing Ink

Following these directions, you can write a secret message and have it reappear.

Materials

- table salt
- small art brush
- water
- black construction paper (one per student)
- oven (Supervision is needed for this part.)

Directions

1. Warm the oven to 150° F (66° C).

2. Add approximately three teaspoons (15 mL) of salt to a ¼ cup (60 mL) water. (Salt will settle to the bottom.)

3. Use the brush to stir the salt solution at the bottom.

4. Use the brush to write a message on the piece of black construction paper.

5. Make sure to stir the salt solution with the brush before making each letter. This will help make a clear letter.

6. Turn the oven off and place the paper in the oven on a wire rack.

7. Allow the paper to heat for approximately five minutes or until the paper is dry. The message will appear as shiny white letters.

Keeping Time

The first clocks, made in the 14th century for kings, were terribly inaccurate and only had one hand. The hand of the clock moved in the same direction as the shadow of the sundial in the northern hemisphere (hence, the direction "clockwise"). Before these clocks were invented, people kept track of long periods of time on a sundial and shorter periods with an hourglass.

Use the directions below to help you make a sand-filled hourglass.

Materials

- two equal-sized salad dressing or small soda bottles that are narrow at the top and wide on the bottom
- sand to almost fill one bottle
- a piece of clear packing tape
- small funnel
- stopwatch

Directions

1. Remove the labels from the bottles.
2. Thoroughly wash and dry the bottles.
3. Fill one of the bottles with sand, using the funnel.
4. Tape the other bottle to the top—upside down—so that the necks are joined.
5. When the bottles are turned upside down, the sand will drain downward. Use a stopwatch to keep track of the time it takes for the sand to completely drain down.
6. Compare your times with other students' hourglasses.

Extensions

- A larger version of an hourglass can be made by using two 2-liter soda bottles and a threaded pipe fixture (available at a hardware store). Compare the times between the smaller and larger versions.

- You may also want to experiment with a simple sundial by driving a stick into the ground and marking off the hours.

Catapults

Catapults were huge machines that could shoot arrows or hurl rocks with great force. Used by the Ancient Greeks, catapult design changed little through the conquests of the Roman Empire and the battles of medieval Europe.

For one type of catapult, the *mangonel*, a huge spoon was wound back and then released, hurling a rock through the air. Another type, the *ballista*, was a large, mounted crossbow that shot heavy spears. The ballista was sometimes used during a siege to guard the exits of a castle so that people could not come out. A final type of catapult, the *trebuchet*, was like a giant seesaw with a heavy weight on one side and a rock in a sling on the other side. When the heavy arm dropped, the lighter end launched its rock against the castle. Sometimes attacking armies threw the bodies of dead animals into the castle walls, hoping to spread disease.

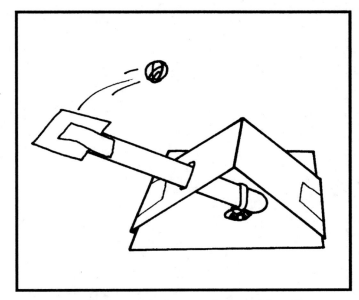

Materials

- 3 pieces of cardboard cut in these approximate dimensions: 3" x 3" (8 cm x 8 cm), 2" x 4" (5 cm x 10 cm), and 1" (2.54 cm) square
- craft stick
- rubber band
- tape

Directions

1. Fold the 2" x 4" (5 cm x 10 cm) piece of cardboard so that the length is cut in half. Make a small slit in one of the halves. (Make sure the slit is big enough for the craft stick to move through freely.)

2. Tape the 1" square to one end of the craft stick.

3. Place the other end of the craft stick through the slit on the folded piece of cardboard.

4. Cut the rubber band and tie one end to the end of the craft stick that was placed through the slit.

5. Poke a hole through the middle of the 3" x 3" (8 cm x 8 cm) piece of cardboard.

6. Pull the free end of the rubber band through the hole on the 3" x 3" (8 cm x 8 cm) piece of cardboard. Tape it securely to the bottom. Make sure the rubber band is taut.

7. Tape your folded cardboard piece to the base (as shown in the picture above).

8. Adjust the rubber band as needed.

9. Try flinging small pieces of wadded paper or pasta with your catapult. Have a contest outside to see which ones shoot the farthest and which others are most accurate. (**Note:** Catapults should be used only under close supervision.)

Medieval Clothing

mantle

In Roman times, most people wore clothes that were wrapped around and tied like a bathrobe. In the Middle Ages, clothes began to be cut and sewn to fit, looking more like our clothes today. Since wash days were few, having lots of clothes began to be important to nobles. Many had large chests full of fine clothing. Clothes were made from a variety of fabrics. For everyday wear, clothes were made out of linen and different blends of wool. For more formal wear, there were softer clothes made of silk, satin, and velvet.

The typical lord might wear soft linen underwear, wool or silk stockings, and a white linen shirt. For more formal times, he might wear a loose, sleeveless outer garment called a *mantle,* which was made from an expensive fabric and often lined with squirrel fur.

Wealthy ladies were very particular about their clothes. They tried hard to keep up with the latest French designs. They often wore dresses that tightly fit their upper bodies and arms and had long, flowing skirts. Women also wore capes, shawls, and furs to keep them warm in the winter. The most spectacular part of a lady's outfit was always her headdress. One type, the *barbette,* looked like a giant cone with a piece of silk hanging down across her back and shoulder. A more modest type of headdress was the *wimple,* a long strip of fabric that was wrapped around the head, chin, and neck. Young single women sometimes wore their hair loose, but married women were expected to keep their hair covered as a sign of modesty.

Common people were far less picky about what they wore. They needed something that was going to keep the heat in and the dirt out. Lower-class women usually wore clothes that were handed down from other family members or cast off by the lady of the manor. Dresses were usually made from a rough wool. A working man might have worn high leather boots, stockings that came up to his waist, a long-sleeve shirt, a belt, and a straw hat.

barbette

Medieval Clothing *(cont.)*

Directions: Complete the chart below by answering the following questions: How are each of the following materials made? Would they have been used to make clothes in the Middle Ages?

Material	Made How?	Worn in the Middle Ages?
acrylic		
burlap		
canvas		
cotton		
leather		
linen		
nylon		
plastic		
polyester		
rayon		
satin		
silk		
velvet		
wool		

Comparison Chart

Directions: Use the spaces below to think about some of the ways that our world today is different from the world of the Middle Ages. For each situation, there may be more than one correct answer.

Situation	Middle Ages	Today
Telling time		
Dating and marriage		
Medical treatment		
Washing clothes		
Educational opportunities		
Travel		
Storing food		
Fixing food		
Clothing		
Entertainment		
Money and taxes		
Getting news		

What other differences can you think of?

_____

_____

_____

_____

The Story of Last Names

A long time ago, four men named Thomas lived in a little town. That was the only name any of them had. In those days, only kings and nobles had last names; most men and women had only first names.

Because the men had the same name, here's how people told them apart. One Thomas had a father named John, so he was called "Thomas, John's son." Another Thomas, a baker, was called "Thomas the Baker." The third Thomas had light-colored hair, so he was known as "Thomas the White." And the fourth Thomas lived next to the village green, so he was known to everyone as "Thomas of the Green."

Time went on. Thomas the Baker married a girl named Elaine. She became known as "Elaine, Thomas the Baker's wife." They had a little boy named John, and he was known as "John, Thomas the Baker's son." But after a while, people got tired of saying all those words. So they simply called Thomas the Baker, "Thomas Baker." His wife became Elaine Baker, and their son was John Baker.

That's how last names came to be. People took their fathers' first names, the names of their fathers' jobs, the names of the places where they lived, or names that told how they looked. They put these names after their first names. When a man married, his wife and children took his last name. Sometimes, a widow or single woman might adopt children and give them her last name. So, today, our last names can tell us something about the people we got them from long ago.

Is your last name on one of the following lists? Here are some examples of *patronymics*, last names that come from first names:

Adding *son* or *sen*	Adding *s*	Adding *es, ez,* or *is*
Andersen	Fredricks	Davis
Davidson	Matthews	Harris
Jackson	Phillips	Hernandez
Johnson	Roberts	Hughes
Robertson	Stephens	Jones
Wilson	Walters	Rodriguez

People who spoke different languages sometimes added *sohn, wicz, vich,* or *ak* to the end of a name. All of these mean "son." People from some countries put *son* in front of their fathers' names. *Mac, Mc,* and *Fitz* all mean "son of."

Here are examples of some last names that came from the jobs that people held:

Blacksmith	Cart Driver	Making Bread
Ferraro	Carter	Baker
Herrera	Porter	Baxter
Kovacs	Wagner	Fournier
Kowalski	**Grinding Wheat**	Shroeder
MacGowan	Miller	**Making Clothes**
Schmitt	Molinaro	Schneider
Schmitz	Mueller	Snider
Smith	Sarto	Taylor

The Story of Last Names *(cont.)*

Here are some last names that were taken from the places where people lived:

By a Hill		Near a Small Forest
Barrows	Strass	Atwood
Downing	Streeter	DuBois
Downs	**By a Stream**	Holt
Hill	Arroyo	Hurst
Hillman	Beck	Shaw
Hull	Brooks	Silva
Knowles	Burns	Wood and Woods
Law	Rivera	
Lowe		**By a Castle**
Peck	**By a Grassy Field**	Borg
	Field and Fields	Burke
By a Main Road	Lee	Castello
Estrada	Mead	Castillo
Lane	Meadows	Zamechi
	Vega	

Here are some names that were taken from the way people looked:

White Hair	New Person	Curly Hair
Bannon	Doran	Cassidy
Blanchard	Dowell	Krause
Weiss	Doyle	Kruse
White	Newcomb	Rizzo
Whitehead	Newman	
Whitlock		**Tall Person**
Whitman	**Short Person**	Lang
Wise	Bass	Long
	Basset	Longfellow
Red Hair	Hoch	
Flynn	Kline and Klein	**Happy Person**
Reed and Reid	Short	Gay
Roth	Small	Merriman
Russell		Murray

Here are some names that described animal characteristics:

Wolf	Fox	Kinds of Birds
Lupo	Fox	Bird and Byrd
Wolf and Wolfe	Todd	Coe
	Volpe	Cox
Deer		Crane
Buck	**Bear**	Crow and Crowe
Hart	Baer	Garza
Hirsh		Hahn
Roe	**Lion**	Ortega
	Leon	Vogel
Dragon	Loewe	
Drake	Lyon and Lyons	

What's in a Name?

During Middle Age times, most people did not have last names. Several people in a town might be known simply as "Richard" or "Mary." As time went on, *surnames* (last names) were added to clear up the confusion. These original surnames came from descriptions of the persons, fathers' or mothers' first names, the places they lived, how they looked, or what occupations they had.

What surnames might these people have had?

1. Your first name is Elizabeth, and your father's name is John.

   Elizabeth _____

2. Your first name is John, and you tend sheep for the king.

   John _____

3. Your first name is David, and you take care of the king's hunting birds.

   David _____

4. Your first name is Geoffrey. Your father is dead. Your mother's name is Catherine, and she works as a cook at the castle.

   Geoffrey _____

5. Your first name is Joshua, and people know you for your white hair and beard.

   Joshua _____

6. Your first name is Elaine. Your father's name is Paul, and he shoes horses.

   Elaine _____

7. Your first name is Rachel. Your father is very tall and works doing odd jobs at the castle.

   Rachel _____

8. Your first name is Mary. You live on the main road through the town.

   Mary _____

9. Your first name is Harold, and you live close to the open field where you sell fruit on market days.

   Harold _____

10. Pick a new surname for yourself based on where you live, what you like to do, or a parent's name.

_____   _____
YOUR (REAL) FIRST NAME   YOUR NEW SURNAME

Making of a Knight

Only a boy of noble birth could become a knight. When he was about seven years old, he might begin his training by moving to the castle of an important friend or relative and become a *page.* Here he practiced archery, fencing, and horse riding in mock battles with other boys. Pages were also taught the customs of knighthood and learned how to be gentle and polite. Most pages were not taught to read or write because people did not think that these were necessary. Pages usually had a long list of chores around the castle, including serving dinner.

When the boy turned 14, he could become a *squire,* an assistant to a knight. As a squire, he learned how to care for armor and horses. Squires also practiced using weapons like bows, swords, and lances. Squires often followed their masters into battle, helping them with their armor, shield, and weapons. They also might care for their masters if they were wounded or fell off a horse.

Squires who worked hard and proved their bravery could become knights when they were 21 years old. Only knights could grant knighthood to a squire. They did this in a ceremony called a *dubbing.* The squire knelt on the ground, and the knight tapped him on each shoulder with his sword and said, "I dub you knight." Later on, dubbing became more elaborate. The day before, the squire would take a long bath and put on a white tunic as a symbol of his purity. He then spent a night awake in the chapel, thinking and praying. Later, ceremonies sometimes included parties and gifts, too.

Although knights were men of war, they were also governed by a code of honor called *chivalry.* A knight was supposed to be courageous in battle, fight according to certain rules, keep his promises, and defend the church. Chivalry also included rules for gentlemanly conduct toward women. Some knights worked full time for certain kings. Knight-errants rode from place to place defending those who needed help.

Making of a Knight *(cont.)*

Directions: Before becoming a knight, a boy had to spend years as both a page and a squire. Use the boxes below to draw pictures for each of the steps toward knighthood, and make a list of things that the person was expected to do.

Page

Picture   **Jobs**

_____

_____

_____

_____

_____

Squire

Picture   **Jobs**

_____

_____

_____

_____

_____

Knight

Picture   **Jobs**

_____

_____

_____

_____

_____

Armor

Chain Mail

Most knights and soldiers who could afford it wore armor during the Middle Ages. When William of Normandy invaded England in 1066 A.D., all his horsemen wore *chain mail,* an armor made of metal rings linked together. Chain mail served as the major form of protection. The suits of chain mail covered the body of a knight from head to foot and provided protection against lances, arrows, and swords. Due mainly to this advantage, he was able to defeat the English whose only protections were large kite-shaped shields. From this time on, horsemen began to wear this type of armor.

chain mail

Weapons

For mounted knights, the weapons of choice were the sword and crossbow. Invented by the Chinese, a crossbow was made by attaching a small, stiff bow crossways to a handle. The crossbow was somewhat clumsier than the longbows used by footsoldiers, but the metal "bolts" it shot could penetrate the armor. Another favorite weapon of the knight was a metal ball attached to the end of a club, called a *mace*. Over time, a chain and spikes were added to the ball to increase its ability to smash through armor. Swung effectively, this type of mace could cause great damage.

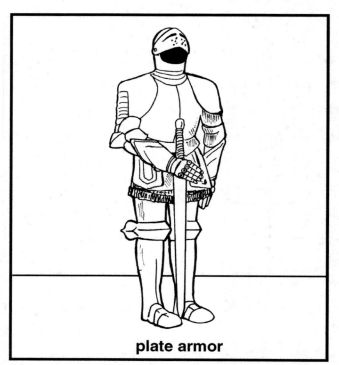

plate armor

Plate Armor

Over the next 400 years, weapons began to be larger and more powerful, and knights were forced to switch from chain mail to armor made of metal plates sewn together. This type, called *plate armor,* was much heavier and more awkward, but it provided better protection against weapons like the battle ax and crossbow.

By the end of the Middle Ages, gunpowder had made armor obsolete. Armor could be made thick enough to protect against a gunshot, but it was so heavy that most soldiers refused to wear it.

Armor (cont.)

Directions: Label the parts on the plate armor below. Choose a shield and two weapons that you would like to have and add them to the picture.

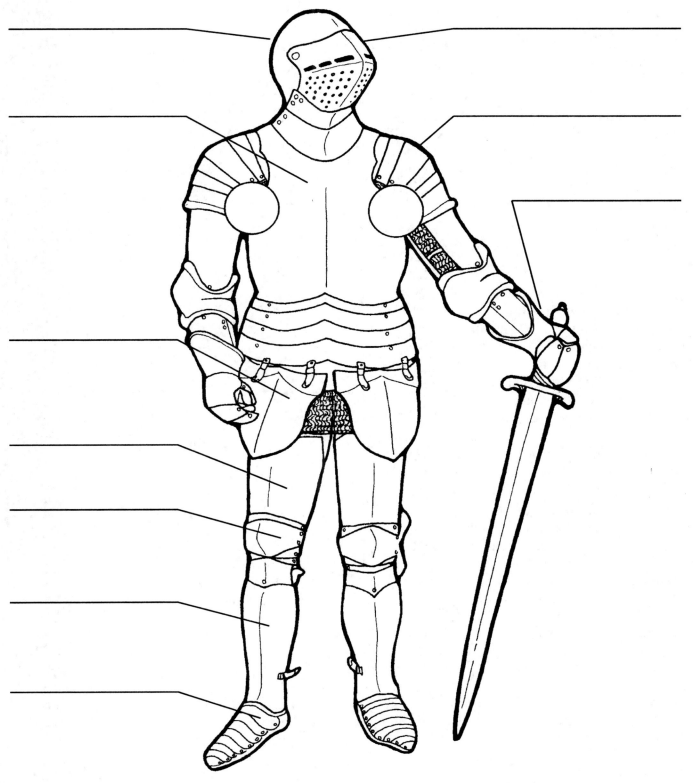

The Crusades

In the early Middle Ages, the city of Jerusalem was ruled by friendly Muslims who allowed Christian travelers from Europe to visit. Some Christians, called *pilgrims,* made the dangerous journey over thousands of miles to see the place where Jesus had lived. Shortly after 1000 A.D., a different group of Muslims conquered Jerusalem and closed the city to outsiders. Christians in Europe were outraged.

The *Pope* (the head of the church) declared a holy war and called upon knights to travel to Jerusalem and free the city. The Pope was hoping that this Crusade would re-open the city to Christian travelers. He also hoped that a holy war would get rid of knights who were causing trouble at home.

Beginning in 1095, thousands of knights and ordinary people joined this first *Crusade.* Many died from disease and sickness over the long journey to the city of Jerusalem. Others froze to death or drowned when they crossed the Mediterranean Sea. The soldiers in this First Crusade conquered Jerusalem, but the next year the Muslims recaptured the city.

Over the next 200 years, there were seven more Crusades. Each Crusade was unique, but all of them were failures. In 1189, Richard the Lion-Hearted led the Third Crusade, leaving his younger brother John in charge of England. (This is the setting for the Robin Hood legends.) On his way back, Richard was captured and held for two years until his mother could raise the ransom to free him. The people in another Crusade robbed and killed thousands of people along the way. Others actually attacked the wrong city! The final and most desperate Crusade took place in 1212, when thousands of children from the ages of 10 to 18 began the journey to Jerusalem. The children believed that their strong faith would give them the strength to take back the city.

Unfortunately, very few of them actually reached the Holy Land. Most either died or were captured and sold into slavery along the way. This was a very sad time for people in Europe.

Despite the years of pain and turmoil, the Crusades changed Europe for good. The knights who traveled to Jerusalem brought back goods like spices and silk, which in turn increased trade. More importantly, they gained from the Muslims new ideas about architecture, medicine, mathematics, and science.

Crusader Quest

Christian military expeditions organized mainly to recapture Palestine during the Middle Ages were called the Crusades. The Holy Land, Palestine, was important to Christians because it was the area where Jesus Christ had lived. Muslims took control of it from Christians. Between 1096 and 1270 A.D., the crusaders from Western Europe organized eight major expeditions to try and gain permanent control of the Holy Land.

Directions: Help the crusaders get from England to Jerusalem. See if you can find your way!

The Feudal System

When William invaded England in 1066 A.D., he had a huge task before him. In order to govern the entire country, he began to give plots of land to knights who agreed to support him. At the top of this system, known as *feudalism*, came the king who claimed ownership over all the lands and demanded taxes and knights from all his tenants-in-chief. They, in turn, demanded homage from their knights and the knights from the freemen and villeins. Each group gave services according to the amount of land they owed.

A tenant had to supply his overlord with a fixed number of knights for 40 days a year. If the knights actually had to fight in a war, they might do so for two months. If there was no war, they did 40 days of training or castle-guard duty. In return, the knight received a fee, land on which to live, and usually a substantial manor.

Some knights did not fight but performed a sergeantry, a special task that might involve carrying the king's banner in battle. Some sergeantries were lower down on the social scale, such as Henry de la Wade of Stanton Harcourt, who fed the king's beasts and mowed a hay meadow reputedly containing lions, leopards, camels, and a porcupine. Sergeantries gradually became obsolete when money became more important in the early thirteenth century. By then, kings could afford paid armies.

The lord's protection was a right that vassals could expect to receive in case of war. The lord also acted as a judge and held a court for his vassals. Freemen could appeal to the King's Court against an unjust lord, but Henry II's royal judges and trial by jury helped to undermine the nobles' power.

The king kept special control over some areas. These included the royal manors, royal forests, and towns. Forests were regarded as an important source of sport for the knights and nobles. There were elaborate laws to preserve animals in both royal and ordinary forests. Towns had their own courts and customs; the kings had control over them at first but granted them freedom to pursue these customs so that by the late twelfth century, towns were increasingly independent.

The Feudal System *(cont.)*

King

The king owned all of the land. He made grants of land to his supporters, but in different parts of the country so that no baron could become too powerful. He kept large areas as royal forests and owned the chief towns and the royal manor.

Land and Protection   **Fully Armed Knights**

Tenant-in-Chief

Bishops and abbots ranked with barons as tenants-in-chief. They had to provide the king with a certain number of armed knights, and their followers had to serve him for 40 days a year. They also had to make various money payments. They might be the lords of many manors.

Land and Protection   **Knight Service**

Subtenant

The country was divided into thousands of "knights' fees," each of which had to provide one fully armed knight to serve his overlord or the king. Each of these subtenants would be the lord of a manor.

Land and Protection   **Military and Other Services**

Villein

Villeins received land in return for working on the lord's manor at certain times and making other payments. They could not sell their land.

Serf

Serfs had no land but had to work on the lord's manor at certain times, as well as make other payments.

Making Parchment

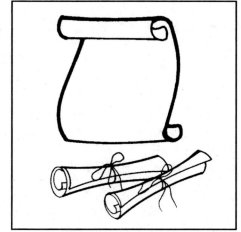

During medieval times, most writing was either done on *vellum*, made from calfskin, or on *parchment*, made from sheepskin. Since most people did not know how to read or write, all manuscripts had to be painstakingly copied by scribes who worked for the church. This made books extremely costly and valuable.

Directions: In this activity, parchment is made by staining construction paper with teabags. When the paper is dry, students will work in pairs, one dictating while the other acting as a scribe. Scribe and speaker will then switch roles so both have an opportunity to write.

Materials

- 9" x 12" (23 cm x 30 cm) piece of white construction paper (one per student)
- 6 oz. (180 mL) foam cups filled with ½ cup (120 mL) of hot water (one per student)
- tea bags (one per student)
- paper towels (to cover work area)

Activity

1. Tear the edges of the construction paper to make it more authentic looking.

2. Heat and distribute ½ cup (120 mL) of hot water in a cup to each student.

3. Instruct students to steep, or soak, the tea bag in the hot water until the bag is cool enough to handle.

4. Place the construction paper on top of the paper towels.

5. Squeeze the tea bag and rub it gently over the construction paper several times. (If students rub the tea bag too hard, the bag might break.)

6. Allow the paper to dry thoroughly before writing on it.

7. Have students imagine that they are people who lived during the Middle Ages and wanted to tell others what the daily life was like. Tell students that most people did not know how to write during this time, and a scribe was needed.

8. Have students work with a partner who will be the scribe. One student will explain what an average day was like. (For example: What time did you wake up? What did you eat? Whom did you see? What happened on the manor?) The other partner will write down the information on a plain piece of paper (rough draft). After that partner finishes a rough draft of the words, the partners will switch places. After both rough drafts are finished, the students will copy each other's words on the piece of parchment that was just made.

Extensions

- Journals can either be rolled and tied with ribbons or bound together in a book to display.
- Have students transcribe limericks or other poetry onto the parchment.

Illuminations

Since manuscripts during the Middle Ages were expensive, they were sometimes beautifully decorated with pictures or designs. Often, gold or silver leaf was used on the first letters to emphasize them. These pictures, designs, and fancy first letters on a page were called *illuminations* since the bright colors and the gold leaf seemed to make the page illuminate or light up. Illuminators were the monks who did the artwork for the manuscripts.

Unique styles of illumination developed in different parts of Europe. For example, there were English and Italian styles of illumination. All these unique styles used six basic kinds of decoration: animals and human figures, branches with leaves or berries, geometric designs, ornamental letters, scrollwork, and braids.

Materials

- plain paper or parchment
- large letter stencils
- colored pens or pencils
- gold or silver ink pens
- dark ink pen
- ruler or straightedge

Activity

1. Sketch or trace the outline of the letter onto the paper.

2. Outline the letter in dark ink.

3. Place a box around the letter using a ruler or straightedge.

4. Add animals, branches and leaves, geometric designs, braids, or scrollwork to add detail to the letter.

5. Use the gold or silver pens to add detail to the decorations.

6. Decorate outside the letter as well.

Making a Mural

Materials

- large pieces of butcher paper
- paints (tempera and watercolors)
- paintbrushes of all sizes
- small jars to hold water
- felt-tip markers
- crayons
- pencils
- sponges that are cut in ½-inch (1.3-cm) squares or rectangles to be used like paintbrushes or paint dabbers
- many pictures of the Middle Ages
- construction paper (optional)
- glue (optional)

Directions

1. Get into small groups and study the pictures of medieval times. Choose one picture to make into a mural.

2. On a large piece of butcher paper, lightly sketch the chosen picture with a pencil. The larger the drawing, the easier it will be to paint.

3. After the sketch is completed, paint the background. Crayon may be used to highlight a specific area. The wax will resist the paint and create a nice effect. Remember, any mistakes can be painted over.

4. After the background is dry, work toward the front of the picture. Paint the foreground. When the entire picture is dry, add detail. Felt-tip markers may be used to highlight specific areas.

5. A 3-D effect can be created by folding construction paper and gluing it to the mural so that it stands away from the background. To get this effect, the mural must be done in stages with the background planned and created first, then the midpoint area, and finally the foreground.

Stained Glass

Churches were the center of life for all villagers, including the lord of the manor. In a day when few people could read and write, stained-glass windows, paintings, and carvings told the stories of the Bible and church saints so that the common people could understand them. As skills in architecture and art improved, windows became very elaborate, especially in the larger abbeys and cathedrals. Some beautifully decorated stained glass windows were called *rose windows.*

Rose windows are large, round windows, usually placed high near the gable at one end of the building. Their patterns are symmetrical. Each section of the rose contains the same shapes, but the individual colors and designs vary. The pieces of colored glass are held in place by strips of black lead called *cames.*

Materials

- black construction paper
- scissors
- glue or glue stick

- small pieces of brightly colored tissue paper or cellophane

- clear cellophane or contact paper (optional)

Directions

1. Cut black construction paper into the shape of a circle, making a frame.

2. Fold the circle into eighths.

3. Cut designs into the folded circle. Be sure to leave enough of the black to frame each shape and hold the window together.

4. Open the circle. Glue pieces of colored tissue paper or cellophane to the back of the frame, taking care to place contrasting colors adjacent to each other.

5. Glue clear cellophane or attach contact paper to the front or laminate these, if desired.

6. Hang your completed rose window in front of a clear glass window so that the light shines through.

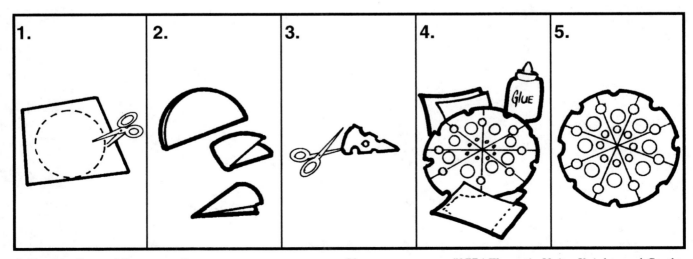

Guild Signs

During the latter part of the Middle Ages, craftsmen organized *guilds* according to the kind of work they did. There were guilds of weavers, candlemakers, blacksmiths, goldsmiths, and shoemakers. Once a guild was formed, no one was allowed to practice that type of work unless they were a member of the guild. Since few people could read or write in the Middle Ages, guild shops had pictures over their doors that told what they sold or did. Some examples are below.

Wheelmakers   **Hatters**   **Candlemakers**   **Painters**   **Pastrymakers**

Directions: What other guilds can you think of? Make a shop sign that advertises something you would like to have sold during the Middle Ages.

Design a Model Castle

Materials

- cardboard carton or box
- blue construction paper
- four paper towel rolls
- tape
- crayons or markers
- scissors
- string
- two metal nuts
- paint

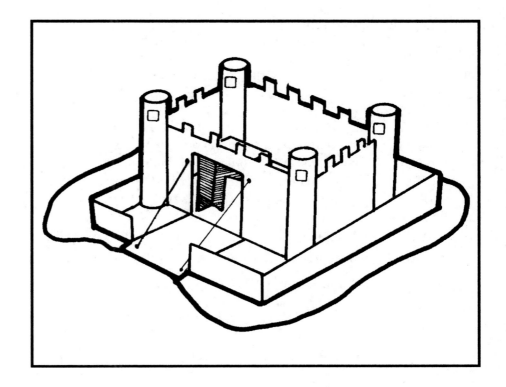

Directions

1. Cut off the top flaps of the box. Around the top of the box, cut evenly spaced notches about $^1/_2$" (1.3 cm) of the way down. Push in every other flap to create battlements.

2. Make a large door in one side of the carton. Leave the bottom of the door attached to form a drawbridge. Poke holes in either side of the door opening and in each side of the top of the door itself. Reinforce the holes with tape, if necessary. Measure enough string to reach from the open drawbridge through the holes and back to the ground.

3. Tie a nut to one end of the string. Feed the other end of the string through one hole on the castle (from the inside outward) and through the drawbridge. The nut provides leverage to keep the drawbridge up. Knot the other end of the string so that it is securely held to the drawbridge. Do the same with the other side and adjust the lengths of the strings so that the door is held all the way up.

4. Use paper towel rolls to create the towers. (Stiff paper can also be rolled up if the castle is large.) Cut notches so that the towers fit the castle. Attach the towers to the castle.

5. Paint or color the castle.

6. Cut a large piece of blue paper as a moat and place it under the castle.

7. Design the inside of the castle with a great hall, stables, shops, and living quarters. Cut arrow loops into the wall for defense. More elaborate castles can be constructed with multiple boxes.

Design Your Own Coin

In the early Middle Ages, people used different types of money, so paying for things became very confusing. Queen Eleanor standardized the system of money in England and put her son Richard's picture on the coins.

Coin designs often show people, places, and animals that are important to the history of a country. Frequently, mottoes are stamped on the coins to express an idea that is important to the people of a country. Take a look at a United States quarter. Who or what is pictured on it? What do the phrases "E Pluribus Unum" and "In God We Trust" mean? Can you remember what the designs are on other coins?

Directions: Now design your own coin. Make sure you include these features in your coin:

- name and amount of your coin
- year the coin was minted
- motto: a brief word or phrase that is important to you

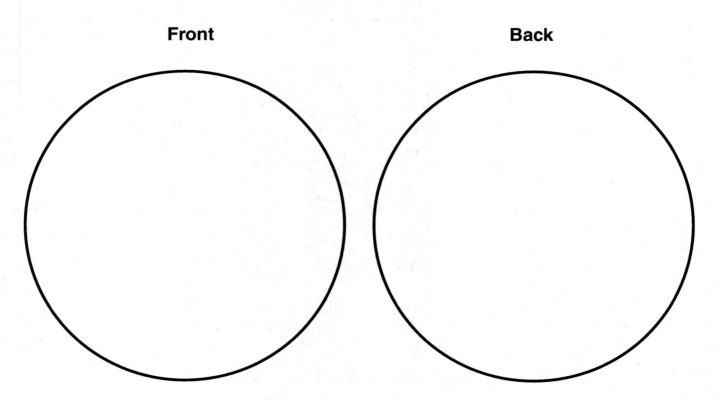

Front   **Back**

Medieval Games

Travel was much less common in the Middle Ages than it is today. In addition, the long cold winters in England meant that people often stayed indoors. Since most people could not read or write, games were a popular form of entertainment. Some games like chess, checkers, and backgammon we still have today. Here are some other Middle Ages activities that you can do with your class.

Blind Man's Bluff (a tagging game)

This game is similar to a standard game of tag except that the person who is "it" is blindfolded. In the Middle Ages, this game is also known as Hoodsman's Blind because the usual blindfold was simply a hood put on backwards with the face opening to the back of the head.

1. Players come as close as possible to "it" without getting caught.
2. A variant of this game is called Jingling, where everybody except "it" is blindfolded. "It" has a string of bells attached to his or her foot, and whoever can catch "it" becomes "it" for the next round.

Tom Tidler's Ground (a tagging game)

1. An area is marked out and designated as Tom Tidler's Ground.
2. "It" must stay within the designated area.
3. The other players run in and out of Tom Tidler's ground and try to avoid getting tagged. Whomever Tom Tidler tags first becomes the new Tom Tidler.

How Many Miles to London? (a tagging game)

1. "It" is blindfolded.
2. All players stand in a line and ask "it" for directions. "It" tells them how many paces forward, backward, left, or right they must go.
3. "It" is led to the starting point and must follow his or her own directions.
4. When "it" is where he or she thinks the other players are, he or she must try to touch one. Players are allowed to duck and sway to avoid "its" touch but must not move their feet.
5. Any player who is tagged or moves to avoid being tagged is "it" for the next game.

Bone Ace (a card game)

This game is a predecessor to blackjack. The object is to get a combination of cards as close to 31 as possible without going over.

1. Use a standard deck of 52 cards.
2. The dealer goes around to each player and asks whether he or she wants to "stick" or "have it." If the player wishes to stick, the dealer goes to the next player. If the player wants to "have it," the dealer gives the player another card.
3. This continues until players decide to "stick" or go over 31, in which case they are out.
4. Number cards are worth their number of points, and face cards are worth 10. An ace is worth one.

Medieval Games *(cont.)*

Nine Men's Morris (a board game)

Use the game board below to play with another person. The object of the game is to capture or block the other person's pieces or "men." Each person needs nine or ten marking pieces, which must be different from his or her opponent.

1. One player begins by placing one of his or her men on the board at any intersection point. Each player, in turn, places a man on an intersection not already occupied.

2. Players try to get three of their own men in a straight line along one of the lines on the board. This is called a mill. The player may then pound (remove) one enemy piece—but not part of a mill, unless no other piece is available.

3. Each player has nine turns to place his or her men on the board.

4. The players take turns trying to make mills and pound the other player's men. Mills may be broken and remade. Men move from existing positions to any adjoining vacant point of intersection and may take pieces by jumping over an enemy to a vacant spot beyond.

5. The game continues until one player is reduced to two men or until one player cannot move. With only three pieces on the board, a player may jump to any vacant place on the board.

The Death of the Middle Ages (and Birth of a New Age)

By the 1400s, two movements had begun which greatly changed the face of Europe. In the North, many thought that the Catholic Church had become corrupt and needed change. This was called the *Reformation*. Writers and artists encouraged people to think for themselves about God. In the South, other writers and artists who made up the *Renaissance* discovered knowledge that had been forgotten for a thousand years. People took a new interest in science, art, writing, and mathematics. These two movements marked the end of the *Middle Ages*, the period of time between the Roman Empire and the Reformation and Renaissance.

Technology and education were greatly changed. Soldiers coming back from the Crusades brought back knowledge from other lands. Before the invention of the printing press, all books had to be copied by hand, one at a time. Afterwards, books could be produced much more cheaply and easily. Many schools were founded, and more people became educated.

The discovery of gunpowder, brought back from the Far East, completely changed warfare. Armor that could protect from bullets was simply too heavy to wear, and stone walls offered little protection against cannon blasts. Lords began to move into smaller, more comfortable houses, and many castles were abandoned. For wars, kings began to use paid soldiers rather than knights.

Later that century, some Europeans set sail in search of new trade routes to India and the Middle East. One explorer, Christopher Columbus, crossed the Atlantic and claimed America for the Spanish king and queen.

Questions

1. List some of the inventions of the 1400s and 1500s. _____

    _____

    _____

2. How did the inventions change life for the common person? _____

    _____

    _____

3. What new forms of government replaced feudalism in Europe? _____

    _____

    _____

Medieval Post Test

Directions: See how much you have learned about the Middle Ages. Write **T** if the statement is true and **F** if it is false.

_____ 1. The wimple and barbette were types of armor.

_____ 2. Knights' outfits were called coats of arms.

_____ 3. The strongest part of the castle was called the keep.

_____ 4. Peasants were considered property of the lord and could not leave the manor under any circumstances.

_____ 5. The strong entrance gate to a castle was called a palisade.

_____ 6. The raised platform in the great hall was called a dais.

_____ 7. When eating, visitors of less importance sat below the salt.

_____ 8. The early Middle Ages were called the Dark Ages.

_____ 9. Moats were good places for fishing.

_____ 10. Chain mail was the main method of communication during the Middle Ages.

Directions: Write the correct answer on each line.

11. The wooden fence that surrounded an early castle was called a _____.

12. A combat between two knights on horseback was called a _____.

13. A knight's code of honorable behavior was called _____.

14. The mangonel and ballista were types of _____.

15. The main room of the castle was called the _____.

16. The castle entertainer was called a _____.

17. The eight attempts to liberate the city of Jerusalem from the Muslims were called the _____

_____.

18. Before becoming a knight, a boy had to spend time as a _____.

19. The most secure part of a castle was called a _____.

20. Morning stars and maces were types of _____.

A Medieval Festival

Manors hosted elaborate festivals in the great hall or in an open area near the castle. Outside festivals were set up like street fairs with booths lining both sides of an open area. Individual areas might be designated as game booths, craft stalls, and an open-air theatre. Food was plentifully served and elegantly displayed. Inside festivals were more modest but still included an abundance of food, entertainment, and games after dinner.

Directions: Use the ideas on the following pages to plan your own medieval festival. Choose a lord and lady to oversee the festivities. Tables can be set up to display art, castles, crafts, and other projects completed by the class. A stage might be used for storytelling, acting, reading of poetry, limericks, journals, or short stories acted out with narration. Food can be served that reflects that time period.

Games

Board games might include chess, checkers, and backgammon. Here are some other events that might be held:

- sack and three-legged races

- watermelon or pie-eating contest

- archery contest (Set up a target about 20 feet away, and have students use bow and arrows made of soft material to try to hit the target.)

- lance accuracy contest (Hang a plastic ring from a string. Each player holds the end of a large paper tube and charges at the ring, letting go of it as he or she passes by. If the lance goes through the ring, the student gets a point.)

- water balloon war (Have students make several water bombs. Divide participants into two groups and designate a safety zone for each. When a student on the opposing side is hit with a bomb while out of the safety zone, he or she is eliminated from the game.)

Jobs

Here are some jobs that students might have during the festival:

- *Serfs:* During a feast, the serfs serve food to the lord and his guests. They carry food from the kitchen to the table and serve stew with a large ladle. They offer fruit and dessert to the guests and clear away plates.

- *Entertainers:* Jesters told stories, did tricks, and juggled for the guests. Minstrels played musical instruments and sang. Still other students can be designated to read their poetry or act out a Middle Ages story.

- *Miscellaneous Jobs:* Utensils were not used during this time, so guests used their fingers to eat all foods. Other students can play the role of "ewerers" and circulate with large bowls of water so that guests can wash their hands between meals. The "panter" was the king's personal waiter and saw to his dining needs. In addition to food and drink, the panter also presented the salt shaker to the king.

Food and Feast

Here are some easy recipes for an authentic menu: cheese, pancakes, Yorkshire pudding, Welsh rabbit, beef stew, fruit platter, salad, wassail, bangers, and scones. Keep in mind that during this period there were no utensils, but napkins were provided. Some students can be designated as serfs to serve the guests. Other students can circulate with bowls of water so that guests can wash their hands between meals.

Cheese and Pancakes

Cut cheese into blocks and serve with bread or crackers. Pancake mixes are available at the supermarket. It is often easiest to get the mixes in which you only have to add water.

Yorkshire Pudding

- ½ cup (120 mL) all-purpose flour
- 1 teaspoon (5 mL) baking powder
- ¼ teaspoon (1.25 mL) salt
- pinch of pepper
- 1 egg
- 1 cup (240 mL) milk
- 2 tablespoons (30 mL) lard or vegetable shortening

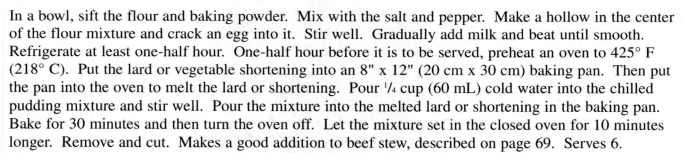

In a bowl, sift the flour and baking powder. Mix with the salt and pepper. Make a hollow in the center of the flour mixture and crack an egg into it. Stir well. Gradually add milk and beat until smooth. Refrigerate at least one-half hour. One-half hour before it is to be served, preheat an oven to 425° F (218° C). Put the lard or vegetable shortening into an 8" x 12" (20 cm x 30 cm) baking pan. Then put the pan into the oven to melt the lard or shortening. Pour ¼ cup (60 mL) cold water into the chilled pudding mixture and stir well. Pour the mixture into the melted lard or shortening in the baking pan. Bake for 30 minutes and then turn the oven off. Let the mixture set in the closed oven for 10 minutes longer. Remove and cut. Makes a good addition to beef stew, described on page 69. Serves 6.

Welsh Rabbit (also called Rarebit)

- two slices of white bread
- sliced or grated Cheddar cheese
- broiler

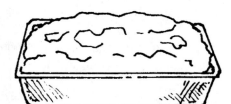

Preheat the broiler. Toast the slices of bread on one side. Turn them over and toast them very lightly on the other side. When slices are just starting to turn brown, take the broiler pan out and top the bread with a thick layer of sliced or grated cheese. Put the pan back and toast the slices until the cheese is bubbling and half melted. Be careful not to burn the cheese. Eat while hot. Serves 2.

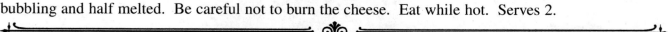

Food and Feast *(cont.)*

Beef Stew

- 2 lbs. (900 g) stewing beef, cut into cubes
- two 8 oz. (225 g) jars beef gravy
- salt, pepper, and other herbs of choice
- onions (optional)

Mix the beef and gravy in a large Crockpot®. Add the seasoning and herbs to taste. Add cut up onions, if desired. Cook on high for 4 hours or until meat is tender.

Fruit Platter

- oranges
- apples
- pears
- grapes

Wash, dry, and slice oranges, apples, and pears. Students can arrange them on a plate with a cluster of grapes in the center or on the side.

Salad

- 2 bunches watercress
- 2 bunches of leafy greens (lettuce and/or spinach)
- 1 medium leek, finely sliced
- 6 spring onions or scallions, finely chopped
- 1 large handful of fresh parsley, separated into small sprigs
- rosemary, sage, thyme, and chopped mint
- salt and pepper
- 2–3 tablespoons (30–45 mL) vinegar
- 4–5 tablespoons (60–75 mL) olive oil

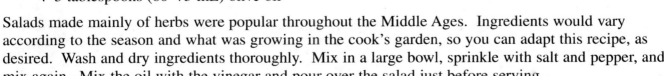

Salads made mainly of herbs were popular throughout the Middle Ages. Ingredients would vary according to the season and what was growing in the cook's garden, so you can adapt this recipe, as desired. Wash and dry ingredients thoroughly. Mix in a large bowl, sprinkle with salt and pepper, and mix again. Mix the oil with the vinegar and pour over the salad just before serving.

Food and Feast *(cont.)*

Wassail

- 2 quarts (1.9 L) apple cider
- 2 cups (480 mL) cranberry juice
- ½ cup (120 mL) brown sugar
- 3 sticks of cinnamon
- ½ teaspoon (2.5 mL) each of ground ginger and allspice
- ½ teaspoon (2.5 mL) ground mace
- 1 large orange, cut into eighths and pierced with whole cloves

Pour all ingredients into a large Crockpot®. Cover and cook for 1 hour on high, stirring occasionally. Then cook on low for 4 hours. Serves 12.

Bangers

- thick rolls (one roll per person)
- Polish sausages or other thick sausage the length of the roll (one per person)
- thinly sliced onions (½ onion per person)
- mustard (1 tablespoon /15 mL per person)
- 1 tablespoon (15 mL) butter or lard

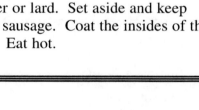

Sauté the onions until golden brown in 1 tablespoon (15 mL) of butter or lard. Set aside and keep warm while you roast or boil the sausage. Open the rolls to hold the sausage. Coat the insides of the rolls with mustard, place a sausage in each roll, and top with onions. Eat hot.

Scones

- 2 cups (480 mL) all-purpose flour
- 2 teaspoons (10 mL) baking powder
- ½ teaspoon (2.5 mL) salt
- 4 tablespoons (60 mL) lard or vegetable shortening
- ¼ cup (60 mL) sugar
- ¼ to ½ cup (60 mL to 120 mL) currants or raisins
- ¼ cup (60 mL) milk or buttermilk

Preheat the oven to 425° F (218° C). In a large bowl, sift the flour, baking powder, and salt. Thoroughly mix in lard or vegetable shortening with your fingers. Then add the sugar and currants or raisins. Mix well. Stir in enough milk to form a stiff dough. On a lightly floured surface, roll dough out until it is ¾ inch (2 cm) thick. Cut into 2-inch (5-cm) circles. Place on a greased and floured cookie sheet and bake in the middle of the oven for about 10 minutes or until the tops are light golden brown. Serve warm with butter and jam or whipped cream. Makes 12–16 scones.

Research Project

Students can learn about the Middle Ages by researching the people who significantly influenced that time. If students will be working in cooperative groups, they might choose to research broader topics. Provide reference books and other materials for students to use. Some materials are suggested at the end of this book. Set aside one area of the classroom as a projects center and/or use the media center for research time. Finished reports can be presented to the class, posted on a wall or bulletin board, or presented at the Medieval Festival.

A *biography* should place the individual in the context of medieval times and demonstrate how he or she influenced history. A *topical study* should cover the topic and connect it to life in the Middle Ages.

Suggested historical figures to research for a biography include the following:

Joan of Arc

King Henry I
Henry II
Leif Erickson
Joan of Arc
St. Francis
Richard the Lion-Hearted
John ("the Lackland")
Gutenberg
Botticelli
Charlemagne
Chaucer
Dante
St. Bernard
St. Gregory I
Marco Polo
William of Normandy
St. Thomas Aquinas
St. Augustine

Dante Alighieri

For topical or group projects, students might research topics such as these:

castle construction	life in the castle
castle defense	life in the town
the Crusades	knighthood
religious holidays	medieval clothing
the role of women	weapons
the guild system	the Inquisition
medieval art	chivalry and courtly love
the Church	food and food preparation
medicine	

Vocabulary Game

Directions: Find out how much students have learned after completing *Knights and Castles*. Use the vocabulary words below to play a class vocabulary bingo game. Give each student a blank bingo grid. Have students place one word in each space on the grid. Students may place the words in any order. Then, randomly choose and read the vocabulary definitions. Students place markers over the words that match the definitions read. A student wins by covering a row or column of words.

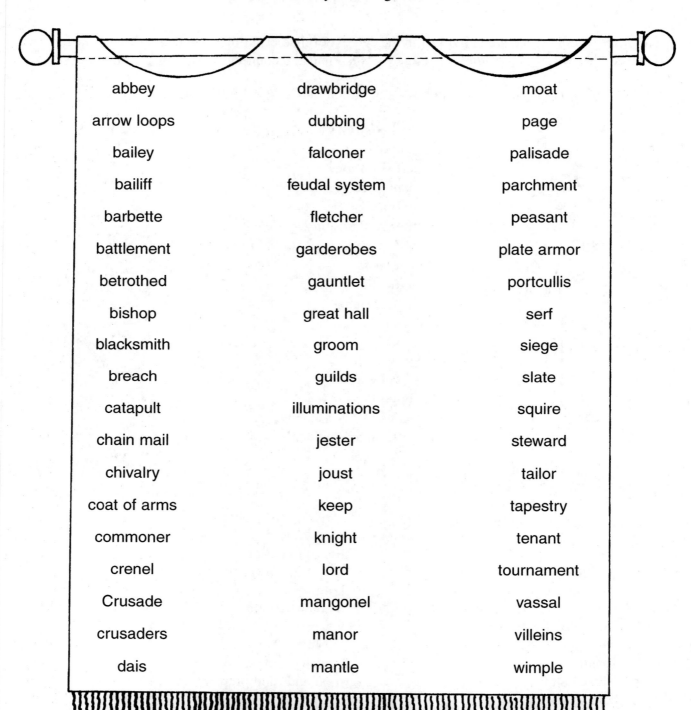

abbey	drawbridge	moat
arrow loops	dubbing	page
bailey	falconer	palisade
bailiff	feudal system	parchment
barbette	fletcher	peasant
battlement	garderobes	plate armor
betrothed	gauntlet	portcullis
bishop	great hall	serf
blacksmith	groom	siege
breach	guilds	slate
catapult	illuminations	squire
chain mail	jester	steward
chivalry	joust	tailor
coat of arms	keep	tapestry
commoner	knight	tenant
crenel	lord	tournament
Crusade	mangonel	vassal
crusaders	manor	villeins
dais	mantle	wimple

Bulletin Board and Classroom Decoration Ideas

Bulletin Board

Bulletin boards can be used to create interest in the subject, graph the progress of the class, or display work that students have done. Bulletin boards reflect the class's interests and creativity.

Cover the background of the bulletin board with butcher paper, art tissue, metallic gift wrap, or cellophane. The background should enhance the display rather than detract from it.

Copy any of the pictures or maps in this book on an overhead transparency or use an opaque projector. Shine the image on the bulletin board and trace with a marker. For an added effect, do not trace the image with a pen but staple, tape, or glue yarn onto the board in the pattern of the shape. Other clip art pictures are easily downloaded from the Internet sites noted in the bibliography section of this book (page 78). The basic bulletin board shape can be used as a base for mounting any of the creative projects described in this book.

Classroom Decoration

In addition, the environment of the classroom can add enthusiasm as students study the unit. Cover bookcases and walls with white or brown butcher paper. Have students paint murals of scenes from medieval life (e.g., a town or forest scene) on the bulletin boards. On other paper-covered sections, have students measure and paint gray blocks to represent the stone blocks of the castle. Another group can paint or construct a giant bonfire to symbolize the one that would have been used to keep residents warm in the great hall. A final group can work on a banner to welcome guests to your kingdom. Post students' parchment writings on the wall and attach stained glass artwork to windows. Tape coats of arms to the walls. To complete the atmosphere, arrange the desks in a circle to symbolize the Round Table and tape "Lord ___" or "Lady ___" name tags to the backs of students' chairs.

Scroll

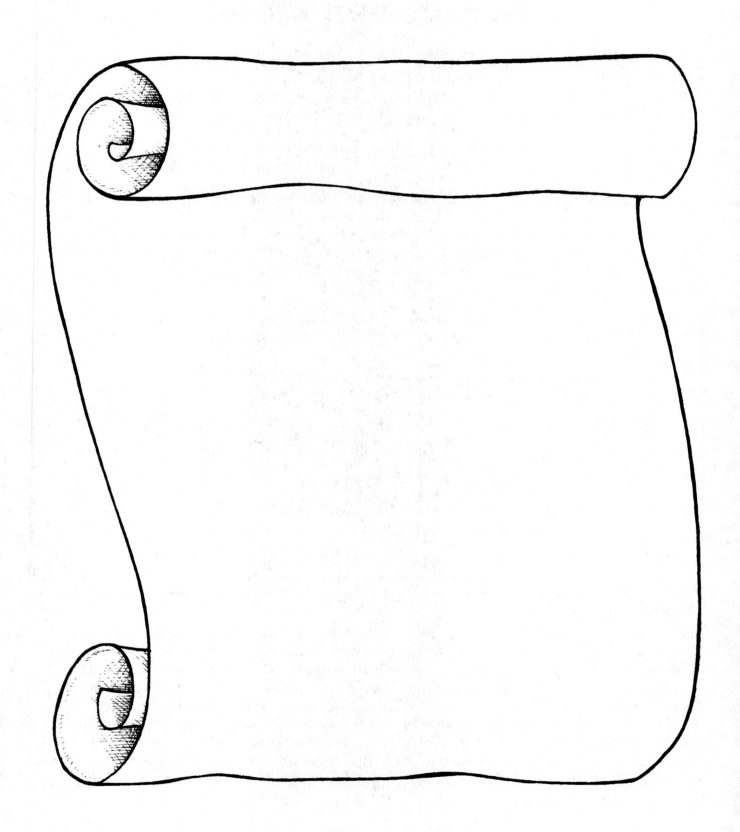

74

Medieval Europe Map in 1360

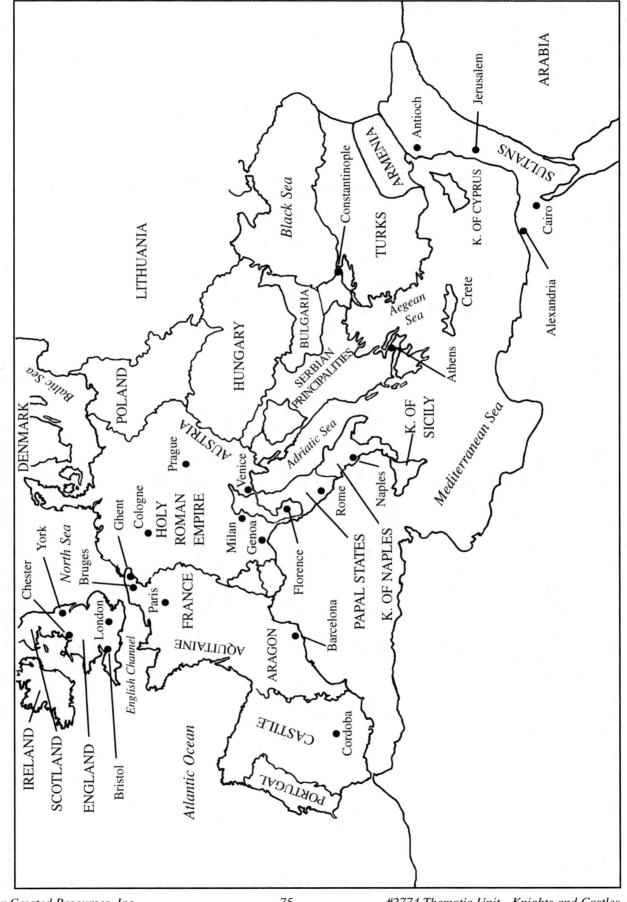

Invitation and Award

Your presence is requested at a
medieval feast to be held in celebration of
our completion of the
Knights and Castles history unit.
The festival will be held
on _____ at _____.
R.S.V.P. by_____

_____
(Signed)

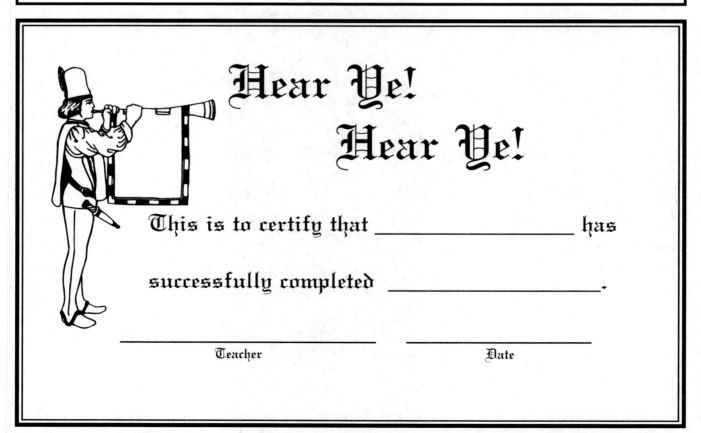

Hear Ye! Hear Ye!

This is to certify that _____ has

successfully completed _____.

_____   _____
Teacher   Date

Bibliography

Fiction

Bulla, Clyde R. *The Sword in the Tree*. HarperCollins, 1988.

Ceswick, Paul. *Robin Hood*. Atheneum, 1984.

Chaucer, Geoffrey. *The Canterbury Tales* (adapted by Selina Hastings). Holt, 1988.

De Angeli, Marguerite. *The Door in the Wall*. Yearling Books, 1990.

Fleischman, Sid. *The Whipping Boy*. Troll Associates, 1989.

Graham, Kenneth. *The Reluctant Dragon*. Henry Holt, 1988.

Gray, Elizabeth Jane. *Adam of the Road*. Viking, 1987.

Green, Roger Lancelyn. *King Arthur and His Knights of the Round Table*. Puffin Books, 1995.

Gross, Gwen. *Knights of the Round Table*. Random House, 1993.

Jones, Terry. *Nicobobinus*. Bedrick, 1986.

MacDonald, Fiona. *A Medieval Castle*. Bedrick, 1993.

MacDonald, Fiona. *A Medieval Cathedral*. Bedrick, 1991.

McGovern, Ann. *Robin Hood of Sherwood Forest*. Apple, 1991.

Miles, Bernard. *Robin Hood: His Life and Legend*. Macmillan, 1979.

Pyle, Howard. *The Merry Adventures of Robin Hood*. Signet, 1991.

Rogosky, Barbara. *Rapunzel*. Holiday House, 1987.

San Souci, Robert D. *Young Guinevere*. Doubleday, 1996.

San Souci, Robert D. *Young Lancelot*. Doubleday, 1998.

San Souci, Robert D. *Young Merlin*. Doubleday, 1996.

Scott, Sir Walter. *Ivanhoe*. New American Library, 1987.

Stanley, Diane. *Petrosinella: A Neapolitan Rapunzel*. Puffin Books, 1997.

Stevenson, Robert Louis. *The Black Arrow: A Tale of the Two Roses*. Atheneum, 1987.

Talbot, Hudson. *King Arthur: Sword in the Stone*. Morrow, William & Company, 1991.

Twain, Mark. *A Connecticut Yankee in King Arthur's Court*. New American Library, 1990.

Watson, Richard Jesse. *Tom Thumb*. Harcourt Brace, 1993.

Wood, Audrey. *King Bidgood's in the Bathtub*. Harcourt Brace, 1985.

Nonfiction

Aliki. *A Medieval Feast*. HarperTrophy, 1986.

Biesty, Stephen and Roger Platt. *Stephen Biesty's Cross-Sections Castle*. D. K. Publishing, 1994.

Byam, Michele. *Eyewitness Books: Arms & Armor*. Alfred A. Knopf, 1988.

Gravett, Christopher. *Eyewitness Books: Castle*. Alfred A. Knopf, 1994.

Gravett, Christopher. *Eyewitness Books: Knight*. Alfred A. Knopf, 1993.

Hart, Avery and Paul Mantell. *Knights & Castles: 50 Hands-On Activities to Experience the Middle Ages*. Williamson, 1998.

Hindley, Judy. *The Time Traveller Book of Knights and Castles*. Usborne Publishing Ltd., 1976.

Hollister, C. Warren. *Medieval Europe: A Short History*. McGraw Hill, 1997.

Howarth, Sarah. *See Through History: The Middle Ages*. Viking, 1993.

Hunt, Jonathan. *Illuminations*. Aladdin, 1993.

Langley, Andrew. *Eyewitness Books: Medieval Life*. Alfred A. Knopf, 1996.

Macaulay, David. *Castle*. Houghton Mifflin, 1977.

Milliken, Linda. *Medieval Times Activity Book*. Edupress, 1995.

Osband, Gillian. *Castles*. Orchard, 1991.

Robbins, Mari Lu. *A Literature Unit for Adam of the Road*. Teacher Created Resources, 1995.

Ross, Cynthia. *Medieval Times*. Teacher Created Resources, 1992.

Wilson, Lynda Duffy. *A Literature Unit for Catherine, Called Birdy*. Teacher Created Resources, 1998.

Bibliography *(cont.)*

Online Sources

http://www.yourchildlearns.com/castle.htm
Directions for building your own medieval castle.

http://tqjunior.advanced.org/4051/
A children's learning tour about castles and medieval times.

http://www.kyrene.k12.az.us/schools/Brisas/sunda/ma/mahome.htm
Information on castles and the lives of knights and noblemen.

http://www.kidscastle.si.edu/
A Smithsonian Magazine site where students can read the latest articles, post messages, and play games.

http://dev.eyecon.com/marcia/gothic/index.html
A simple medieval game.

http://users.aol.com/gerekr/medieval.html
General and advanced information on costumes, arts, and culture of the Middle Ages.

http://www.nyu.edu/gsas/dept/history/internet/geograph/europe/medieval/
An index of medieval and renaissance history links.

http://www.camelotintl.com/heritage/warrior.html
Catalogs the great leaders and fighters of the Middle Ages, as well as related topics.

http://www.fordham.edu/halsall/sbook.html
Accesses essays, documents, images, and other medieval resources.

http://www.shss.montclair.edu/english/furr/medieval.html
Includes reviews and links to Web sites dealing with the history and literature of the Middle Ages and additional information about medieval art, culture, and music.

http://www.chainmail.com/chainmall/cteach2.htm
Instructions for making a set of chain mail using pliers and a set of rings.

http://www.lepg.org/warfare.htm
Link to specific historical information about major battles and related information.

http://history.idbsu.edu/westciv/plague/
A guide to the causes and effects of the bubonic plague in Europe during the Middle Ages.

Software

Castle Explorer. DK Media. 95 Madison Ave., New York, NY 10016.
Castles II: Siege and Conquest. Interplay Productions. 16815 Von Karman Ave., Irvine, CA 92606.
Eyewitness: History of the World. DK Media. 95 Madison Ave., New York, NY 10016.

Videos

The Adventures of Robin Hood. MGM/UA Home Video, 1938.
A Connecticut Yankee in King Arthur's Court. MCA/Universal Home Video, 1949.
Camelot. Warner Home Video, 1967.
Castle. PBS Home Video, 1983.
Ivanhoe. MGM/Universal Home Video, 1952.
A Kid in King Arthur's Court. Walt Disney, 1995.
Knights and Armor. A & E Home Entertainment, 1994.
Our Musical Heritage: Music of the Middle Ages. Hollywood Select Videos, 1994.
The Prince and the Pauper. MGM/UA Home Video, 1937.
The Princess Bride. Cary Elwes Nelson Entertainment, 1987.
Robin Hood. Walt Disney, 1973.
The Sword in the Stone. Walt Disney, 1963.

Answer Key

Page 9

1. The journal begins in 1290 in the village of Stonebridge, in the shire of Lincoln, England.

2. She dislikes him and calls him a beast.

3. There is great hatred toward the Jews. The king has banished all Jews from the country, and Birdy's father does not want to give them shelter as they leave.

4. Birdy sews linens, dispenses medicine, makes soap, and picks maggots from meat.

5. She is jealous of Aelis and George and fears they will fall in love.

6. The tub is being used as a table until spring.

7. (See the entry for November 23.) She cannot imagine her father as a handsome, young knight.

8. She cuts up a lute string and sprinkles it on a dish of creamed herring. The strings wiggle around like worms and upset the guests at the feast. The cook yells at Birdy, and she is sent to her room.

9. Before the hanging, she is eager to go. After attending and seeing the young criminals, she is physically ill and has to leave.

10. He doesn't have to do women's chores, can sleep outside, and doesn't have anyone telling him what to do.

11. Answers will vary.

12. The ink freezes, the food is the same every day, and it is hard for the animals.

13. Answers will vary. (Sample answer: When children misbehave, it is like a punishment for the parents.)

14. Birdy thinks that the spell she cast on George and Aelis has worked.

15. Lent is the religious season before Easter. It is a time of fasting, dark colors, and no celebrations.

16. Answers will vary. (Sample answer: Agnes does not like gossip, telling stories, or dance. Agnes finds fault with all of Birdy's actions and thinks she talks too much.)

17. Answers will vary.

18. Answers will vary. (Sample answer: Birdy thinks Ethelfritha gets to do whatever she wants. She wears strange clothes, laughs and cries a lot, can drink more than Birdy's father, and orders all the servants around.)

19. On May Day, people dance around a maypole, wash their faces with dew, and eat at a feast. A village boy and girl are named king and queen of May. There are also games and athletic contests.

20. Answers will vary.

21. Birdy feels sorry for George's dead wife and child, she helps an ant take food to its colony, and she tries to locate a cottage for Meg and Alf.

22. The peddler is punished by being put in the stocks. A necklace of rotten fish is placed around his neck, and people throw rotten food at him.

23. Most saints are men and gain their sainthood through a variety of accomplishments.

24. Answers will vary.

25. He asks the abbot, who agrees, to take care of the bear. He also uses some of his own money to help Birdy.

26. Birdy uses her dowry from Shaggy Beard to buy the bear's freedom, even though it will mean that she must marry him.

27. Answers will vary.

Page 10

1.–3. Answers will vary.

Page 13

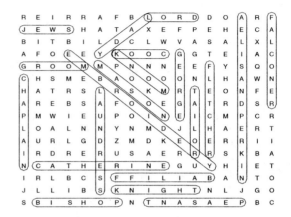

Page 14

1.–4. Answers will vary.

Page 15

Answers will vary.

Page 20

1. The main characters in the first scene are Eleanor, Matilda, William, and Abbot Suger.

2. He fears that she will be old, ugly, or stupid.

3. Eleanor's father is very bold in his prayer. He seems to think of God as a partner and offers to donate money to a church if God will let him defeat his enemies.

4. The church has not been consecrated yet. It does not belong to God.

5. They are cousins.

6. Louis rode at the rear while Eleanor rode at the front. Louis traveled simply while Eleanor dressed elegantly and brought along boxes of candles, cosmetics, and clothing.

7. The caravan was long, and the luggage of Eleanor and her ladies took up half the space. The mountain peaks made it difficult to travel in a straight line. The women often had to be carried because they could not handle their horses on the mountains. Eleanor and Louis fought about where they should camp for the night.

8. Raymond was handsome and daring. He shared Eleanor's taste for expensive furnishings, dress, and art.

9. The "Truce of God" was an order from the Pope that said no one was allowed to attack the lands of any lord who was on a Crusade. If landowners knew that their property was going to be protected while they were away, they would be more likely to go. Also, if they thought someone was about to attack them, they might have gone to postpone the war.

10. Eleanor refurnished her castles with linens, embroideries, and gold plate. She provided a home for all musicians and poets in the land.

11. They sailed across the English Channel through a storm, even though Eleanor was pregnant.

Answer Key (cont.)

Page 20 (cont.)

12. Their children were William, Henry, Matilda, Richard, Geoffrey, Eleanor, Joanna, and John.

13. Henry introduced trial by jury, allowed people to appeal directly to the king's court, and had clerks record what happened. This law became known as the English Common Law.

14. Matilda thinks that Thomas will choose to serve God rather than Henry.

15. Neck verses, according to Henry, were the six verses that you needed to recite to prove that you were a member of the clergy so you could "save your neck."

16. She went at Henry's request to help keep peace in the region. She also went because she was jealous of Henry's mistress, Rosamond Clifford.

17. The "Courts of Love" were rules for how men and women should behave toward one another. They were organized because the young people, who were guests at Eleanor's court, were getting out of hand.

18. Because he was the youngest son, he did not inherit any land. Henry asked each of the other children to give him a portion of their land.

19. She changed the histories to make them more interesting. She asked poets to rewrite the stories so that the knights were more interesting, the ladies more beautiful, and the court more noble.

20. Young Henry gave away his clothing and wore the ring his father sent to make peace.

21. Eleanor was 67 when she got out of prison. She felt that her real life began at that age after her husbands and two of her sons had already died.

22. She freed the monks from the responsibility of keeping the king's horses. She standardized the system of weights and measures. She standardized the system of coins and had Richard's face engraved on the coins. She finally gave a lavish festival celebrating Henry's coronation.

23. She granted charters to the towns to make the people more responsible for their own government and defense. By doing this, she hoped that they would support John.

24. John signed the Magna Carta, agreeing that he would treat his subjects fairly and deal with them according to the law. The lords forced John to sign it because of the heavy taxes that he had imposed and the lands he had lost in France.

Page 22

1.–4. Answers will vary.

Page 26

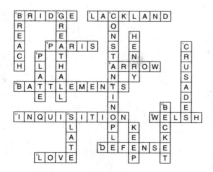

Page 33

1. DAIS	10. KEEP
2. JOUST	11. JESTER
3. PALISADE	12. BATTLEMENT
4. MAIL	13. CRENELS
5. GREAT HALL	14. CATAPULT

Bonus Word: GUILD   Bonus Word: SLATE

6. WIMPLE	15. MANOR
7. TOURNAMENT	16. CHIVALRY
8. BAILIFF	17. VILLEIN
9. PORTCULLIS	18. CHAPEL
	19. GARDEROBE

Bonus Word: MOAT

Bonus Words: CHAIN MAIL

Page 47

Answers will vary.

Page 51

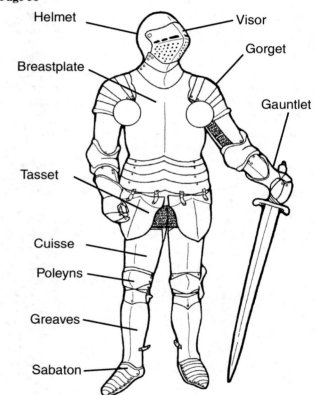

Page 65

1.–3. Answers will vary.

Page 66

1. F		11.	palisade
2. T		12.	joust
3. T		13.	chivalry
4. F		14.	catapults
5. F		15.	great hall
6. T		16.	jester
7. T		17.	Crusades
8. T		18.	page/squire
9. F		19.	keep
10. F		20.	weapons